DATE DUE

POINT, CLICK, and $AVE

Mashup Mom's
Guide to Saving and Making Money Online

Rachel Singer Gordon

CyberAge Books

Medford, New Jersey

First printing, 2010

Point, Click, and Save: Mashup Mom's Guide to Saving and Making Money Online

Copyright © 2010 by Rachel Singer Gordon

Publisher's Note: The author and publisher have taken care in preparation of this book but make no expressed or implied warranty of any kind and assume no responsibility for errors or omissions. No liability is assumed for incidental or consequential damages in connection with or arising out of the use of the information or programs contained herein.

Many of the designations used by manufacturers and sellers to distinguish their products are claimed as trademarks. Where those designations appear in this book and Information Today, Inc., was aware of a trademark claim, the designations have been printed with initial capital letters.

Library of Congress Cataloging-in-Publication Data

Gordon, Rachel Singer.
  Point, click, and save : mashup mom's guide to saving and making money online / Rachel Singer Gordon. -- 1st ed.
    p. cm.
  Includes index.
  ISBN 978-0-910965-86-6
  1. Stay-at-home mothers. 2. Online social networks. 3. Teleshopping. 4. Electronic commerce. 5. Thriftiness. I. Title.
  HQ759.46G67 2010
  658.8'72--dc22

2010007825

Printed and bound in the United States of America

President and CEO: Thomas H. Hogan, Sr.
Editor-in-Chief and Publisher: John B. Bryans
Managing Editor: Amy M. Reeve
VP Graphics and Production: M. Heide Dengler
Book Designer: Kara Mia Jalkowski
Cover Designer: Denise Erickson

www.infotoday.com

Contents

Acknowledgments

This book would not have been possible without the wonderful readers at MashupMom.com (www.mashupmom.com) who generously shared their stories with me. Thanks are also due to John Bryans at Information Today, Inc., who took a chance on a very different book from this former librarian. And I couldn't have done it without my family, who has come along more or less happily on this mashed up journey. Thanks to you all—and to everyone else who provided support and encouragement along the way!

About the Blog
www.mashupmom.com

After you've digested the information in *Point, Click, and Save,* come join me at MashupMom.com. This blog focuses on money-saving and money-making strategies for moms—and everyone else!

Here are just a few of the things you'll find on the site:

- Weekly store deals

- Freebies

- Work-at-home stories and info

- Online deals

- Printable coupons

… and much, much more.

MashupMom.com can be your next step in putting your new money-saving, money-making ideas into practice. So come be a part of the Mashup Mom community! I look forward to seeing you and reading your comments there.

Introduction

Hi, I'm Rachel, author of *Point, Click, and Save* and the original Mashup Mom. But really, you might be a mashup mom, too—you just don't know it yet! And if you're not a mashup mom yet, you can definitely become one. Read on to find out how. What is a mashup mom, anyway? Here's the deal: Online, a *mashup* refers to a website that combines info from at least two different places to create something completely new—it "mashes it up." In real life, many moms (and dads, and everyone else) also combine different things to create something new: We mix, or *mash up,* money-making and thriftiness strategies to create a whole new model of motherhood.

Mashup moms don't fit neatly into the two camps of working or stay-at-home mothers. We're all working, right? And mashup moms often *work* by *saving* money. Putting in the time to strategize, coupon, and plan is a job in itself, and many stay-at-home moms also bring in an income through side work. We supplement our family's income by selling items online. We take on freelance or contract assignments or provide consulting services to organizations in our pre-child profession. We run a home day care or give piano lessons or sell Pampered Chef or create crafts for Etsy; we answer online surveys or blog or serve as experts on answer sites. Part-time or freelance work, mashed up with savvy saving strategies, helps make staying at home both workable and desirable. Mashup moms know that we need both pieces of the puzzle.

When you become a mashup mom, you'll also feel more able to ride out today's turbulent economic times. Learning how to save and make money from home is even more important when we're facing everything from sky-high gas prices to double-digit increases in grocery staples to collapsing financial institutions. How do mashup moms make and save money, even when the economy is imploding? We use technology as it was originally intended: to save us time and money. We use the internet to:

- Find *legitimate* ways to make money from home

- Connect with others, finding support and learning from other people's experiences

- Comparison shop, print coupons, and identify other immediate money-saving strategies

- Make money online with the savvy use of everything from survey sites to affiliate networks

- Remain active in and connected with our former profession—and our new one

- Find information on everything we buy, from researching major purchases to comparing interest rates

- Use online resources to save for major purchases, save for college, and save for the future

Those of us who aren't yet mashup moms would like to be. I worked as a librarian for 10 years before deciding to work for myself. Now, I'm a freelance writer, blogger, workshop leader, and editor—and a work-at-home mother with two small children. Other moms ask me all the time,

"How can I do what *you* do?" But they usually don't want to be a writer or an editor themselves. What they really want to know are the answers to the questions we all have: How can I realistically combine home and work life? How can I find legitimate work-at-home opportunities? How can I afford to leave full-time outside employment? How can I compensate for the loss of outside income? In other cases, their families have been personally affected by the ongoing economic downturn, so they wonder how to make—and save—money at home to help weather the storm.

The following chapters will help you answer all of these questions and more. You'll find candid insights from other work-at-home, money-saving moms, combined with solid and practical advice on using online resources to let you work at home—while spending less, organizing both your work and your home life, and saving more on everyday purchases. You'll hear from moms who see saving hundreds of dollars per month *as* their part-time jobs, from moms whose savings strategies allow them to scale back to part-time, at-home work, and from moms who just thrive on working at home. The internet lets us pursue these types of opportunities as never before, and you'll soon discover dozens of exciting online resources and strategies for building your *own* mashed-up life!

In today's uncertain economic times, as the cost of everything from day care to gas to food continues to skyrocket, a mashup mom's role in ensuring the stability and security of her family becomes ever more essential. It's my hope that *Point, Click, and Save* will help you find the right balance for yourself and your family, and I look forward to hearing your comments and ideas. Please stop by to connect with me and other mashup moms at MashupMom.com (www.mashupmom.com).

Rachel Singer Gordon
rachel@mashupmom.com
Blog: www.mashupmom.com
Twitter: @mashupmom
Facebook: www.facebook.com/pages/Mashup-Mom/203016711636

1

Let's Get Started

I don't have to tell you: We've been living through some seriously scary economic times, and we all could use some reassurance that we and our families will make it through OK. Even better, we want to know that we can *do* something to help ourselves make it through, that we can take steps to help reduce the impact of the down economy on ourselves and our family. So fight back with *Point, Click, and Save*! I will give you the strategies you need to both *save* and *make* money from home. I will share thoughts and stories from moms just like you who have made this work, and I will pass along ways to use online resources to mash up the right balance for your family, helping you survive tough economic times—and maybe even have some fun doing it.

As with anything else, the road to saving and making money from home starts by just taking the first step. Any little bit you save, and any little bit you earn, puts you that much closer to your goal. Think of it as being a lot like dieting (but easier). Just as when we try to lose weight, we tend to get overwhelmed when we focus on the big picture. Any of you who have tried to diet know what I mean: It's *so very easy* to get discouraged before you even start. We think: "I have so much weight to lose" or "It's impossible" or "I'll never be able to do it" or "It will take forever." So we have one more piece of cake, one more bowl of ice cream, one more bag of chips, figuring that it doesn't matter in the grand scheme of things anyway.

This is just like our thinking about money. We think, "We're living *this* much beyond our means each month" or "We have a *pile* of credit card debt to pay off" or "We'll *never* be able to afford a house" or "We might as well buy whatever we want because *we're already in so deep* that it doesn't matter anyway." When we get bogged down in this type of thinking, we never begin to take the steps that will eventually let us get ahead. As with dieting, learning how to save takes time and starts with the simple decision to move forward from this point.

Because this book focuses on using online resources to help us change our patterns and our thinking, let me tell you right now about one of my favorites: Get Rich Slowly (www.getrichslowly.org/blog). Let's focus on one word in that title: *slowly.* We can look at saving and making money from home in the same way we look at losing weight: Slow and steady wins the race. We would all love to have that get-rich-quick (or get-thin-quick) magic, but real life doesn't work that way. It took time to get where we are, so it takes time to get ourselves out of it. It took time to build our bad shopping habits, so it will take time to re-pattern ourselves into using good ones. If you use the advice in the following chapters, though, you will begin to see savings almost immediately—and these savings will build faster as you gain confidence and learn the ropes.

MY STORY

So what's my story?

I had always been pretty good at living within my means—but this was probably because I was never seriously challenged until we had kids. Before my first son was born, 7 years ago, I worked full-time, my husband worked full-time, and we were a pretty typical dual-income couple. We bought what we wanted without really worrying about it, I never clipped coupons, and we ate out *a lot*. I always figured that I would go back to work full-time after we had kids and continue working my way up the ladder.

Then everything changed. On my way up that ladder, I found out we were expecting child No. 1, and all of a sudden, the thought of going back to work full-time didn't sit quite as well as it always had before. So we sat down and thought about our budget (and about the cost of full-time day care), and we decided we could make it if I worked part-time after our son was born. That worked out very well for a few years. Because I worked weekends and from home, we didn't have to pay for child care (although this arrangement made for some short weekends). While working part-time, though, I started doing some freelance work on the side: writing, speaking, and editing. I found that my freelance work was both a lot more fun than my "day job" and required less time away from my family. So in the spring of 2005, I decided to throw caution to the wind and strike out entirely on my own. This decision made us start to think a little harder about how we spent our money, but we still didn't make any drastic changes.

The next year, though, we started the adoption process for our second son. This made it very clear that we needed to change our ways further. Although I was bringing in income on the side and my husband still had a full-time job, we really had to take a good hard look at what we were spending and what we were saving. Not only was the adoption process expensive but we were adding another member to the family, and we would have to start buying diapers and formula (both insanely expensive) again. So I started looking for the best ways to save. I stumbled across a few deal sites online and was amazed by the amount of information available. Right on the internet, people were explaining, step-by-step, how to save money, how to make money, and how to change long-held patterns.

I took notes, collected coupons, and made my first, nervous trip to my local Target with my envelope of coupons and scribbled ideas. I walked out of the store with 60 percent savings—and haven't looked back since! In our current economy, I'm happier than ever that I made that leap, and now I want to tell you how you can do it, too. The internet lets people share information like never before, and wonderful people from all over the country take advantage of this opportunity to share their knowledge, their strategies, and the places to find the coupons that make all of this possible. In this book, I share some of these strategies with you and tell you where to look online (and in the real world) to find the best ways of saving and making money for *you*.

BE FRUGAL—BUT DON'T BE CHEAP!

Strategy No. 1: Think about what being *frugal* means to you. I know what you're thinking when you see the word *frugal*—I really do!—but don't let it scare you off. My two rules here are:

- *Frugal* does not mean *cheap*.

- We all need to find the right balance of strategies for ourselves.

Being frugal, as opposed to cheap, means being realistic about what works for you and for your family. It means finding ways to save that don't cause anyone too much stress. What does this mean in practice? Here are some examples.

Books and blogs on frugality often suggest practices that seem extreme to most people, such as making your own laundry detergent or timing your showers. Let me tell you this: I'll be making my own laundry detergent when pigs fly, and I count long, hot showers and baths as two of life's simple (meaning, necessary) pleasures. What I *will* do, though, is strategically match coupons and sales so that I never (and I really do mean *never*) have to pay full price for my laundry detergent. What I will do is wash almost every load of laundry in cold water, which gets clothes just as clean as hot water does and saves me money on every energy bill. What I will do is seek out ways to feed our family's Diet Coke addiction (and my carnivorous husband) as cost-effectively as possible.

The proper balance will differ for everyone. You may find Zen-like contentment in making your own detergent or in turning every bit of acreage into an organic backyard vegetable garden—and more power to you! You may choose to pay higher prices to eat organic dairy, produce, and meat as often as possible; you may have food sensitivities or allergies that require you to follow a special diet; or you may need to purchase extra meat because you follow Dr. Atkins. You may find that name-brand diapers really do fit your baby better or that (like me) you are addicted to Diet Coke and no other brand will do. Balance means that when we save in one area, we have more left to spend on what's important to us. Balance means that we each set our own priorities and that we can't measure ourselves against what other families find works best for them. Balance means that we should ignore media-touted examples of extreme frugality and the unmatchable savings of shopping trips staged for the TV cameras. Frugality means finding the best and easiest ways to save, but it shouldn't ever mean reaching the point where saving becomes impractical or downright painful.

SETTING PRIORITIES

If you stop to think about what's important to you, you will be able to decide where to allocate your precious time and energy. We need to get away from comparing ourselves to other families—how much they earn, how much they save, how many *things* they happen to have—and concentrate instead on what's most important to us and our own families.

How do you establish your own priorities, and how do you determine where the best balance for you might lie? I started by asking myself a series of questions such as, "How important is it to me to work from home?" or "How much do I want to shave off my grocery budget each month?" Your own questions right now might include such things as, "How much debt do I need to pay off?" or "How much do I need to save for my children's college?" or "How long will it realistically take to pay off my own student loans?" or "How will I replenish my lost retirement savings?"

Who needs to think about these things? Everyone! But especially:

- Stay-at-home or out-of-work moms seeking ways to save money, build a career, and bring income into the family

- Stay-at-home or out-of-work dads seeking ways to save or make money in a down economy

- Working moms seeking to scale back and find workable ways of staying home while still staying in touch, being productive, and bringing income into the family

- Work-at-home moms seeking ways to add to their incomes and incorporate savings strategies into their lives

- Not-yet moms—women in the process of starting or deciding when to start a family—who naturally worry about balancing work and home life and about the long-term cost to their careers of removing themselves from the workforce entirely

- Parents worried about the country's economic direction and about maintaining their family's standard of living in uncertain economic times

Recent polls show that more women than men are concerned about their short-term economic security. Go figure! We worry about what we can do to take care of our families, whether we'll have to go back to work, and what to do about ever-increasing grocery prices. Well, the good news is that there *are* things you can do to help combat these worries. Incorporating mashup mom strategies into your own life will definitely help you save— and can also help you find a workable way of staying at or working from home. Listen to self-described Pennsylvania Marine Corps wife, mom of two, and proud birth doula Amy Owen:

> I have always seen this as a part-time job. I joke around with people when I'm out shopping at the stores. They see my coupon binder (it's about 4-inches thick), and they say, "Wow, you are organized." And I say, "Yep. It's the only job you can do at home and still watch reality TV at the same time." Some people leave their house to earn money yet save nothing when it comes to shopping. They spend crazy amounts of money on day care, gas, food for their lunches, and whatever else accumulates while working outside the home. I do the opposite. I work whatever hours I want at home to save big money for my family. To me, it seems backwards to do it any other way. Some women work part-time jobs. For what they earn in salary, I save in coupons and deal hunting, *and* I get to transport my kids to their activities and be on call for them.

Throughout the following chapters, you will hear stories from other women like Amy who have been able to mash up the life that's right for them and their families.

I find it encouraging just *how many* women already run their own businesses or make money on the side. Today's economy encourages people to think about different ways to do so in their own lives, giving some of us the push we need to figure out what it is we'd love to do—and to go for it. There are already more than 10 million woman-owned, home-based businesses in the U.S.!

Working at home, a trend that began even before the current economic crisis, is becoming more and more popular; it rose 23 percent between 1990 and 2000, according to the U.S. Census Bureau. A stressful economic climate only makes more people want to try it for themselves, creatively turning trouble into opportunity by taking the chance to strike out on their own. Think about your own goals, skills, passions, and priorities to see whether working at home is a good option for you, and think about how much time you want to spend working at home for pay. In Chapters 7 and 8, I'll also talk about a number of ways to bring money in on the side without committing to a regular full- or part-time job.

When we think about changing what we do, we also need to evaluate what our job means (or meant) to us. We tend to define ourselves by what we do rather than by who we are. We worry about how others will see us if we remove ourselves from the paid workforce and give up our title or other trappings of on-the-job prestige. This is another time to stop comparing yourself to others. Don't worry about what other people think or do—worry about what works for *you*.

SAVING MONEY VERSUS EARNING MONEY

One of the things to think about when determining your own priorities is how to balance saving and earning money. That balance is exactly what makes a mashup mom! We tend to underestimate the power of saving in our own lives, though, thinking that little bits just don't matter. What's most important to realize here is that, when you save money, your dollar goes further. Let me repeat: When you *save*, your dollar goes *further*. Money saved is actually worth *more* than money earned!

Why should this be? First, when you earn money, you need to deduct both your expenses and the government's share to figure out your actual take-home pay. You must ask yourself what it actually costs for you to work. If you work outside the home, your expenses include everything from child care costs to your investment in a work wardrobe to lunches out to the extra gas you use while commuting every day to the extra money you spend on carryout or convenience foods because you don't have time to cook. Then subtract federal taxes, state taxes, and FICA. Figure in also the cost in time away from your family and the things you could be doing to help save and make money from home. You can use the One Income Calculator from Crown Financial Ministries (www.crown.org/Tools/Calculators/Work_One Income.aspx) to help you figure out exactly how much you're taking home after all is said and done.

So if you're planning on *saving money* to replace the loss of part or all of your outside income, you may need to save less than you think. If you're planning on *earning money* to replace the loss of part or all of your outside income, you may need to earn less than you think *when you combine those earnings with saving strategies!* The exact dollar amount you earn matters less than how much of it you can *keep*. The less you spend, the less you have to earn—if you don't buy it or if you pay much less for it, you don't need to bring in the money to pay for it. Or as Jeff Yeager of Ultimate Cheapskate.com says, "A penny saved is a penny you don't need to earn again!"

The rest of the chapters will give you ideas on both saving and earning, helping you find the right balance for your family.

GETTING YOUR FAMILY ON BOARD

Getting your family on board with any lifestyle change, whether it involves you staying home, taking on new responsibilities, or changing the ways in which you spend money, can be the toughest part. You may need to drag your family kicking and screaming into any change in lifestyle; anything that takes your attention away or that requires a change in eating or buying habits will be difficult for family members to get used to doing.

The best way to get your family on board is by getting them involved. My 7-year-old loves watching the total drop on the register at the store as coupons are scanned, and he's learning lessons there that will stand him in good stead throughout his life: This is why Mom clips coupons. This is why we're buying this particular product instead of Brand Z, whose ad he's seen on TV approximately 1 billion times. This is why Mom and Dad work: to earn money to pay for this food. And this does truly sink in. Some of the most frugal people around now picked up their strategies in their own childhood. Helen T., a newlywed and "cat mom" who enjoys saving money in her free time, explains, "I always remember my mom using coupons while I was growing up. We quickly learned that we had the best chance of getting a 'treat' if it was on sale and mom had a coupon. I was also taught to pay my credit card off each month and to compare prices at multiple stores for big-ticket items."

Here are some strategies that can help get your family on board:

- Make saving into a game. Who can figure out which product is the best deal? Who can cut coupons out the straightest? Who can spot the best sale item in the grocery store this week?

- Combat any sense of deprivation by minimizing change or finding acceptable alternatives. (I'll talk more later about getting name-brand items for free or for pennies on the dollar.)

- Always be on the lookout for kid-friendly deals. I stopped at the store with my oldest son and picked up two Hershey's bars for 2 cents. (I combined a buy-one-get-one-free sale with a buy-one-get-one-free coupon and paid just the tax. Don't worry, we'll go through how to do this later!) On the way out of the store, my son found a penny in the parking lot and exclaimed, "Hey, Mom! Let's go back and buy one more!" Now *that's* some strategic money-saving thinking!

- Make it *fun.* When you make saving a family activity, it becomes a bonding activity.

- Use your savings or experience in finding deals to purchase family-pleasing items you otherwise wouldn't be able to afford.

Get your spouse or significant other on board, too. Money is at the root of many arguments, so don't let it be the root of problems in your relationship. Get the discussion out in the open and decide together to plan to save.

And when you start saving at the store, start showing off the receipts. Examples of just how much you can save with a few simple strategies should convince anyone! Lynn M. from North Canton, Ohio, did just that: "Couponing is definitely a lot of work—I spend about 20 minutes per grocery store flyer with my coupons, looking for the best deals. One day my hubby asked why I waste my time. Once I had everything organized, I had him go shopping with me. He was shocked when I got 15 packages of bacon for 79 cents each."

Why Online?

Why is the *online* part of the making and saving money equation so important? Simply because the internet opens up opportunities to both companies and consumers that we never had before. From printable coupons to online stores to online marketplaces, you can use online resources to maximize your savings and to find ways to bring in extra income. Because there are literally thousands of resources out there, I'll help you find some of the best and identify which ones might be most helpful to you and your family.

Strike the right balance in the time you spend online, too. You can learn to pick and choose the right online activities for yourself, just as you pick and choose the right deals for your family.

Tips and Tricks for Online Success

Free Your Email

When you start to sign up with companies online to print coupons or get sales information—especially with companies you don't know—be smart by setting up a free online email account that you use *only* for your online money-saving activities. The major free email services are:

- Gmail (gmail.google.com)

- Hotmail (www.hotmail.com)

- Yahoo! Mail (mail.yahoo.com)

Go to any of these sites to set up an account, and then use that address whenever you sign up for anything online. This helps protect your real email account from spam and helps you keep your online money-saving activities separate from your personal or business account. Bonus tip: If you're very busy online, feel free to set up multiple accounts for multiple types of activities— one for survey sites, one for freebies, and so on.

Get Involved

Do unto others. Part of being involved in an online community— whether you're talking to other work-at-home moms, bargain-seekers, or both—involves realizing that these are real people on the other side of your screen. *Don't* type things online that you wouldn't say to someone's face. *Do* share the deals and tips you have found, just as others will share with you.

GET ONLINE

You may now (so frugally) be accessing the internet at your local public library, a friend's house, or other public location. This is important: *You will need to have your own computer and internet connection* to take full advantage of this book. While public libraries do offer free access, this access is necessarily limited; there are time limits, and there are limits on what you can install and what you can do. If you only access the internet from a public location, you won't be able to do things like print out coupons, sell items effectively online, take timely advantage of deals, or otherwise maximize the ways you can save and make money online.

So how do you get yourself a cost-effective computer and high-speed internet account? If you are considering a new machine, you will find that computer prices have been dropping over the past few years—great news for all of us! You might also look into one of the new *netbooks*, which offer everything you need to get online in a compact (and much cheaper) package, or check out the refurbished computers at Geeks.com (www.geeks.com) and on manufacturer's sites, including Dell.com. *Refurbs* often come with the same warranties as new computers and can be purchased at substantial savings. You can also check sites such as craigslist (www.craigslist.org) and Freecycle (www.freecycle.org) for used PCs. Although these refurbs or used computers will be slower than newer machines, you may find something that's suitable for your purposes—and you can start putting aside some of the money you're saving toward a faster machine later!

The price of high-speed internet access is also coming down, especially if you "bundle" it with phone, TV, or both. Most cable internet and DSL providers offer introductory packages that include the first few months free and a low guaranteed rate for a year or so. If you already have access or have reached the end of your introductory period, did you know that you can bargain down the price? Here's how: Call your internet provider and ask for the cancellation department. (Don't ask for Customer Service, because those folks are not as likely to be helpful.) Tell the person you reach that you want to find out how to cancel because you're thinking of switching to another provider. Do the research—and really be ready to switch. You will be asked whether there's anything your present provider can do to help you decide to stay—and the conversation gets better for you from there. It costs a lot more for these companies to find a new customer than to make concessions to keep an existing customer, and they know this. We recently reduced our internet bill by $20 per month (that's an extra $240 a year) with just a 10-minute phone call—and this strategy also works well also for things like cable or satellite TV service.

LIFELONG STRATEGIES

Many of us only grudgingly change the way we live when times get tough, yet later we find that these changes have become habits and then useful strategies for the rest of our lives. Some of you may have parents or grandparents who lived through the Great Depression of the 1930s and who developed habits then that served them well throughout the following decades. Similarly, the habits you develop now can serve you well throughout your life. This book and these strategies are not just for use in times of recession—they're for always.

While *Point, Click, and Save* doesn't talk in-depth about topics like getting out of debt or paying down a mortgage (these topics are books in themselves), once you find your way toward a different balance of saving on everyday purchases while bringing in additional income, you might find that you're ready to venture further. Controlling your spending is the first step, and some of the resources in the Recommended Reading section at the end of the book will help you move forward on that journey.

These strategies will also help carry you through if tough economic times directly impact your family. People who have used these savings strategies all along talk about how the down economy just confirms the need to *always* be thoughtful about where we choose to spend our money. Christine S., an Illinois mother of a toddler, explains, "What the downturn has done is further solidify the need to continue to be good stewards of our money and make wise, thought-out decisions in regard to spending, instead of last-minute, *want*-based ones," while mom-of-two Kristine S. says, "I am worried about whether we have enough in savings to handle it if my husband were to lose his job, so I am definitely more focused on trying to ensure my family is safe."

Jaycie, a mom of two who blogs at Coupon Geek (www.coupongeek.net), spells it out best:

> The economy has changed how I value everything in general and how I shop. Any time I buy anything, I ask myself, "Do you truly need this item?" or "What will this purchase possibly prevent me from buying that we may need?" Jobs are becoming scarce, so I try to live like we would should we be down to living off of unemployment alone! I figure it will save us money and if the worst should happen, it wouldn't be such a change in how we live now. And in the meantime, we continue to grow our savings and our retirement/college funds with what we don't spend—or what we save using coupons and finding deals!

Others have been directly impacted by the economic crisis, but their newfound savings strategies have helped them make it through. Jen F., a part-time librarian and mom to two boys, says, "Recently, my husband lost his job. Rather than spend our current income on an exorbitant grocery budget (which it once was), I would much rather spend as little money as possible on groceries so that we have money for other, non-coupon-friendly, expenses, like healthcare." Pam B., mother of two, says, "A while back my husband's hours at work were drastically cut. This newfound way of couponing and stockpiling has allowed us to go on living without having to make too many adjustments or make our sons too miserable. They know we cannot do and have everything we used to, but it is not as bad as it could have been." And Barbara G., a private music teacher, shares this story:

> At the beginning of the year, my husband had to take a $10,000 pay cut to work for a new company—so we went from an already stretched income/budget to even more trimming. Couponing does take a little time and effort to stay organized and on top of things. It's been taking me about 30 to 45 minutes to pull coupons and prepare for a good shopping trip using coupons, and I spend about 2 to 3 hours each week on the computer following the blogs [and] coupon forums and putting my deals together. *But* the items I am able to get from couponing have made it possible to have a smaller grocery budget, saving us money! I am well-stocked with cereal, goodies, condiments, juices, baking items, toiletries, etc. That alone has saved us and helped us to live abundantly!

Now let's start building those strategies by getting into the savings game!

2

Change the Way You Shop

When you want to start saving money at the store, you first have to step
back and take a good hard look at the way you shop. Many of us shop this
way: We think, "What do I feel like for dinner this week?" or "What sounds
good today?" Then we race through the store to buy those products, regardless of whether we're getting a good deal on them. We get distracted by displays and nifty-looking new products and figure we'll give them a try, just
this once. We grab the name brands and sizes we're used to without taking
a minute to compare prices and options. We grab the stuff that's on eye
level without looking more deeply to see whether another item might do
just as well.

Then we realize midweek that we're out of milk, or OJ, or bread, so we
make another little run (or two or three) back to the store—where we never
buy just milk, OJ, or bread. We end each week too many dollars poorer and
ever more frustrated over the rising prices and shrinking sizes of our
favorite items.

While people are using more coupons in these tough economic times,
we are not always using these coupons effectively. Many of us look at the

coupons in the Sunday paper, get frustrated that most of them don't match up with what we are thinking about buying this week, and throw the rest away. I'll talk a lot more in-depth later about just *how* to save money with coupons, but for now, just know that the small savings on each item you buy with coupons can add up very quickly. When you learn how to plan, you will be able to squeeze a *lot* more savings out of those coupon dollars. One of the biggest expenses for most families is food—and, believe it or not, it's the one we can do the most about. Take two to four weeks just to track your expenses at the grocery store. Throw all your receipts into an envelope, add them up, and I guarantee that you will be shocked at the amount. When you calm down, think about how much you want to cut from that total each month.

PLAN TO SAVE

Before you can begin saving with coupons and online resources, you need to change the way you shop. This might seem like a lot of work up front, but once you get into the habit, it simply becomes a way of life. And it's worth the effort to be able to feed your family well in tough economic times—or when you hit the jackpot on savings at the store! When you shop on impulse, you're literally throwing money away. Savvy shoppers can save hundreds of dollars each month simply by putting a bit of planning into the process, and there are, of course, online resources to help with this.

It may take a while to build up a "stockpile" of commonly used items (not to mention a stockpile of coupons), so you will start to see your most dramatic savings after two or three months of playing this game. Don't get frustrated: Again, starting small can build up to major results over time, and you will start to see *some* savings almost immediately. I promise: If you stick with it, the amount you will save will amaze you.

How Do You Know When You're Getting a Good Deal?

Regular grocery shoppers will notice that prices at their local stores seem to fluctuate almost randomly. A box of cereal that's on super saver special for 99 cents one week might go up to $3.95 the next, then drop to $2.50, then pop back up to $3.15, then back down to $1.99. What *you* want to do is ensure that you never, ever have to purchase that box of cereal at that full $3.95 price. You want to buy it as often as possible at the 99-cent sale price—and you want to use a coupon when you do.

This requires a bit of planning, and the secret here is that *grocery store pricing tends to run on 12-week cycles.* That is, almost every item in the store will hit its lowest price about once every three months or so and then will bounce around for the rest of the cycle. (Sometimes it's a 10-week or a 14-week cycle, and sometimes there are seasonal variations, but most items follow these fairly regular price cycles.)

What you want to do is buy enough of a product at its lowest price to last you until it hits that price again. You don't want to run out of a staple in the middle of its sales cycle and find yourself having to buy that item, regardless of what its price happens to be that week. If your favorite cereal is on sale for 99 cents, you might actually buy nine boxes—instead of saying, hey that's a good deal, let me grab one box.

You also want to hold onto coupons for your favorite products until those products go on sale, preferably at their lowest price. Most of us want to run to the store as soon as we see a coupon for a preferred item or brand, but if we wait a bit, we can usually save a lot more. Saving 50 cents on a $3.95 box of cereal is a drop in the bucket, but saving 50 cents on a 99-cent box of cereal is fantastic!

How do you know when items hit their lowest price? In the pre-internet days, savvy shoppers would keep a *price book*. Basically, when they went to the store each week, they would jot down the price of their favorite cereal that day, and then track the price over time to see how it varied and to keep track of the patterns. You can give this a try yourself. Just jot down items, sizes, and prices each week in a notebook, in an Excel spreadsheet, or on a printable template (you can find one at organizedhome.com/printable/houseworks-planner/price-book).

However, there are people online who *do a lot of this for you!* Check out CouponMom.com (www.couponmom.com) or the Grocery Game (www.thegrocerygame.com; this one is a for-pay site) to see the best deals in your local stores each week. You can also follow local deal bloggers, or people who run their own websites devoted to saving money. They'll tell you what the best deals are each week—and where to find the matching coupons. (You'll find out more about these bloggers and where to find them in Chapter 3.)

When you stockpile effectively, you never have to worry about running out of a common item and needing to pay whatever outrageous price your local store happens to be charging for it that day. If you walked into my house today, you would find 10 tubes of toothpaste under the bathroom sink and 15 jars of peanut butter in my pantry. This isn't because I'm crazy (although my family might beg to differ)—it's because I only buy these items when they're at their absolute lowest price, and I buy them with coupons. I'm never going to have to go out and pay $3.50 for a jar of peanut butter or $3 for a tube of toothpaste. Instead, I stocked up when they were nearly free and bought enough to last us until they hit their lowest price again. When we run out of something, we just go into the cabinet and grab a new one instead of running out to the store to replace it.

Just as important, if there are *no* good sales at the store this week, I might skip buying anything but perishables. This is because I stocked up on everything else at its *best* price, so I don't actually *need* to shop. This lets me shop much more strategically. I can easily cook a week's worth of meals (or more) out of my stockpile, and no one would notice the difference. Stockpiling saves you time and gives you many more meal options each week, even if there aren't any good deals at your local stores. It also cuts down on those midweek trips to the store, where many of us are likely to pick up impulse items.

If you have limited storage space, you might want to start just by stockpiling a few of your family's most commonly used items when you see a fantastic deal. For many people, this may include things like cereal, peanut butter, diapers, deodorant, toilet paper, toothpaste, and shampoo. (But think creatively here: Risers can create under-the-bed storage, and over-the-door shelving can turn the insides of closets and cabinets into a pantry.) Organize your items so that those with the earliest expiration dates are in front and keep like items together so that it's easy to see what you have at a glance.

Depending on the types of items you purchase, you may also want to invest in a separate small freezer. Watch craigslist (www.craigslist.com) and garage sales for deals on gently used freezers. We eat meat more often than I'd cook for just myself (that husband of mine is still on Atkins!), so I buy and freeze extra chicken, hamburger, and the like when I see it at a *great* price. I also often buy the large "family packs" for an extra discount, then immediately repackage them into smaller sizes and freeze them when I get home. You can also freeze some types of produce, cheese, even milk (pour out a bit first so the container doesn't burst)—you can stockpile almost anything!

Stockpiling Is Not Hoarding

Never confuse *stockpiling* with *hoarding*. Stockpiling simply means that you build up a big enough supply of commonly used products that you never have to pay full price for them at the store. Stock up more on items when there's a great sale or when they have lengthy expiration dates. For instance, I have more than a year's supply of laundry detergent in my closet right now—but I got all of it for between *free* and $1 per bottle. Now, I never ever have to run out and buy a $7 bottle of laundry detergent but can instead wait out the price cycles until the *next* great sale comes along.

When you hoard items, on the other hand, you buy to excess: more than your family could ever use before the expiration date. When you hoard items, you like to admire them rather than use them. You worry about "using up" one of your 15 jars of pasta sauce or "running out" when you drop below 20 boxes of cereal on the shelf. When you hoard, you have difficulty letting anything go. Try to find the fine line here. If you find yourself storing more than you need, go through your hoard and begin donating it to others.

This difference is hard for some people to understand. When you begin stockpiling items, friends and family may think you are being greedy or that you're even just a little bit nuts—but they may eventually see the light. Megan, a mother of four boys, shares that "I started couponing after I saw an article in the *Chicago Tribune* about a woman in the suburbs with practically a room full of almost free groceries and toiletries. I was a little disgusted, honestly (I thought she was being greedy—I'm realizing that's a common reaction by 'outsiders') but then became curious about how she did it."

How do you stockpile if your budget is already stretched? First, realize that you can't afford not to! Even if you just start out slowly by buying a couple of extra items that are extreme deals each week, you'll start to see your savings build over time. Realize that you will spend *much, much less in the long run* if you spend a little more now. Again, it's like losing weight: Small steps add up!

Every time you go to the store, take the time to browse through your store flyer. If you don't get these in the mail, visit the store's website to view them online. Make a list and attach the coupons you're going to use on each shopping trip. I tend to put my lists in aisle order for the stores I visit most often so I can easily see what I have yet to buy. I'll talk more later about collecting coupons, but once you have a good stash built up, it will be easier to just bring the ones you intend to use on any one visit. Stick them in your checkbook, paperclip them to your list, or just throw them into an envelope before you go to the store. (If you get frustrated when you find unadvertised deals for which you've left the coupons at home, or if you live too far from the store to make follow-up trips, consider using other methods. Find out more about organizing coupons, and life, in Chapter 9.)

How do you decide what you're going to buy and what coupons you're going to use? The best way is by following local bargain-hunting blogs.

Start by visiting The Grocery Gathering at BeCentsAble (www.becentsable. net), which you'll find linked under Grocery Store Deals. Most bargain bloggers write weekly posts about the best upcoming deals at their local grocery stores. The Grocery Gathering links to these posts, letting you know about the latest deals at grocery stores around the country—and letting you find some of the bloggers who cover the stores in your area. Pick your state and then look through its alphabetical lists to find your local stores. Under each, you'll see links to the bloggers that cover that store. Click on through to read about the most current deals and then see what else is on the blog that might be useful. You can also try the Frugal Map at BargainBriana (thefrugalmap.bargainbriana.com). Here, just click on your state on the map to find local bloggers.

A lot of people look at the time they take doing this planning and shopping as a part-time job in itself. Jaycie, mom of two and blogger at Coupon Geek (www.coupongeek.net), explains:

> Couponing is indeed a part-time job for me. To get the best deals, you often need four of a particular coupon. And just simply organizing (and clipping) that kind of paper is a challenge! I then have to be sure I stick within my grocery/household budget but still get enough deals to stockpile to save us money. Each week, I scope out the best deals. I make a game plan of where to go and what coupons I need and then pray for the best—in that all the deals will be available and that the clerks are friendly! Everything just takes time, but it's so worth it! It's incredible how much further I'm able to stretch our money by just taking a little bit of time each week to coupon and find deals.

 Illinois Grocery Deals

Aldi
*My Springfield Mommy

Butera
Couponing As a Way of Life
Couponing for 4

Country Market
*My Springfield Mommy

Cub Foods
Simple Savings Blog

Dierbergs
Clippin' Carie

Dominick's
Couponing for 4

Hy-Vee
Little People Wealth
Penny Pinchin Mom

Jewel
Couponing As a Way of Life
Couponing for 4

Kroger
Mummy Deals

The Grocery Gathering at BeCentsAble

Kristy B. is a mom of three.

I left a high-paying, full-time teaching position to scale back to part-time when our first child was born, and then scaled back even further to full-time stay-at-home mom when our third child was born. With one income instead of two, money started to get tight, and I knew that I needed to make major changes in order to continue to stay at home and save money at the same time. My husband and I are opening a business this fall, and I will be working part-time from home to help out with the business. Starting a new business means we need to be ever more vigilant about our spending habits—and as our children grow and expenses increase during these tough economic times, there is no better time than the present to really focus on how to run a household and save money at the same time. Like everyone else, we have nervously watched our savings decrease and our stocks plummet. Even more frightening, I decided to leave a stable, high-paying job at the same time that the recession was at its worst. We have had no choice but to make some tough decisions on our spending habits and look for ways to save and stretch our dollar.

I do in a way see couponing as a part-time job. I have developed a system where I only will purchase sale items at the grocery store and only items that are truly needed. It helps to stock up on sale items like meat, frozen foods, and toiletries when they are a good deal so I do not have to buy them later at a higher price when I absolutely need them. A bit of planning each week, which I found requires only a few hours, can save literally hundreds at the store on a monthly basis. This enables our family to put money away for larger expenses and luxuries like trips, college savings, and holidays.

Pre-children, I rarely clipped coupons and didn't bat an eyelash at paying full price for clothing and food. I just thought that a box of cereal was supposed to cost $3.99. Now, I would never pay full price for cereal (we go through a box every few days!). Seeing the savings at the end of the month in our checking account has reduced tension in our house and also eased the stress of starting a new business, with its expensive start-up costs. I have even gotten my husband on board—yesterday, in fact, he mentioned that he needed to get some supplies for the business at Office Max. I gave him the 20-percent-off bag to fill from the Sunday paper and a $10-off-$40 coupon I received for signing up with [the Office Max] site. He saved a bundle and was thrilled!

When you're getting started, take it slowly. It is easy to get overwhelmed with wanting to do too much too fast. Change the way you buy groceries, for example. Shop sale items and then plan your weekly menus from there. Find one couponing website you like and thoroughly examine it before you go to the grocery store. Plan, plan, plan before you shop! It may take a while for you to develop a system that you like (how to store/carry/use your coupons), but you will figure it out. I also suggest you find some time to shop alone and not with a few kids in tow. You are more likely to take your time instead of hurrying through the store before a meltdown. Also, shop Sunday through Wednesday. These are the days when the best deals are likely and deal overlaps occur.

MashupMom.com has been a tremendous asset to me as a mom who wants to stretch her family's dollar and to maximize sales without having to do all the labor-intensive research. I simply read the blog each day (or weekly) and plan my shopping trips from there. By saving money, I was able to spend about $30 to buy school supplies (on sale with coupons, of course!) for needy children through our church's back-to-school supply drive. Also, it is very satisfying to give back by donating ["free" items from stores] to local food pantries. You get back what you give!

When you devote time to saving for your family, you are doing them just as much good—or even more—as if you devoted that same time to working outside the home. When you take just a bit of time to plan your shopping and your meals using the many online resources available, you're better able to maximize your savings. Spur-of-the-moment shopping is a killer here. What's useful also about seeing couponing and saving as a part-time job is that this is a job that gives back exactly as much as we put into it. The more time we spend on our planning, the more we can save. This allows you to balance your time and effort with your own family's needs.

The Cost of Loyalty

Our difficulty in saving at the store is made even worse by the fact that we also tend to be brand-loyal to so many products. This is so often just out of sheer habit. Whether we tend to purchase the products we grew up with or have just become accustomed to looking for a particular logo, we get locked into always buying the same brand—even if another brand is on sale for much less and tastes or works pretty much the same. Companies invest a lot of time and energy in ensuring that we remain brand-loyal because our loyalty maximizes their revenue. They spend a lot of money and effort getting their logos in front of us as much as possible and their products at eye level in the grocery store. Start your frugal journey by being aware of their tricks.

Think about instances when it makes sense to be brand-loyal and when it may be *non*sense. Our family, for instance, is brand-loyal in a few areas (that Diet Coke comes to mind). But does it really matter what kind of toothpaste we use, when they all have the same active ingredient? Will the laundry detergent we grew up with really get our clothes that much cleaner than any other brand? Might it even be fun sometimes to try a different kind of deodorant, a different kind of cereal?

I bought Tide religiously for 15 years. Why? Simply because my mother sent me off to college with one of those familiar orange bottles. I never used another brand of laundry detergent until I was in my mid-30s, when one day I stood in the store dithering over the $6.50 bottle of Tide versus the bottle of All right next to it that was on sale for $3.50. It was a tight week, so I reluctantly took the plunge and went with the All. Guess what? My clothes didn't stink! And they still don't, even though I have a mix of several different kinds of detergent in my laundry closet right now—none of which is Tide (sorry, Tide!).

You may not wish to give up brand loyalty completely (some brands really *are* better than others), but instead, take steps to begin saving by dividing that loyalty among several brands. Instead of sticking with one brand of shampoo, you may find there are several that get the job done just as well—and some that you wouldn't touch again with a 10-foot pole. You'll figure out what works for you with a little trial and error, taking small steps now for big savings later. I've found that several brands of laundry detergent work just fine for me, while there are a couple that just don't smell right or don't seem to get the clothes quite as clean. You can look for the best deals on the several brands that work for you and simply avoid the others. The point is that the more flexible you can be in terms of brands, the more you will be able to save.

But What If I Can't Stop Being Brand-Loyal?

All of us will be hopelessly attached to a few favorite brand items, and that's OK. Just realize that if you're brand-loyal in one area, then you'll need to increase your savings in another area to balance this out. Here are a few other strategies that will help.

Join Online Loyalty Programs

A number of companies run online loyalty programs to keep customers involved and buying the same products. Some examples include:

- Accumul8 Rewards (eightoclock.promo.eprize.com/accumul8): Eight O'Clock Coffee lets you record your coffee purchases online and then redeem points for merchandise.

- Pampers' Gifts to Grow (en.giftstogrow.pampers.com/index.html): This is Pampers' loyalty rewards program. Packages of Pampers diapers and wipes contain codes that can be entered online to earn points, which can be redeemed for prizes (mainly children's items).

- LaVicRewards (www.lavicrewards.com): Enter codes found on La Victoria salsa and taco sauce and earn rewards that can be redeemed for printable product coupons, as well as entries into a monthly sweepstakes.

- My Coke Rewards (www.mycokerewards.com): This reward program allows you to enter codes from select Coca-Cola products to earn points. These points can later be redeemed for merchandise, sweepstakes entries, or coupons for more Coke products.

- Stouffer's Dinner Club (dinnerclub.stouffers.com/index. tbapp): Earn points for purchasing Stouffer's products and then turn them in for rewards or donate points to Feeding America. (Thirteen donated points equals one meal for someone in need.)

What are your favorite products? Check inside the packaging for information and codes; visit the product or manufacturer website to see if it runs a similar program. If you're going to be buying the product anyway, you might as well see if you can get something back. On many of these reward sites, prizes also come and go, so hold onto your points until you see something you'd really like to redeem them for.

Make a Point of Contacting Companies

Visit the website of your favorite brand. (It's usually pretty easy to find these with Google; if not, visit the bigger company that makes the product, if there is one. Look on the product's packaging to find its parent company.) Look for a Contact Us link. Fill out the online form or send an email message complimenting the company's product and be sure to include your mailing address.

I run a "Four Companies a Day" series on MashupMom.com, where I contact four companies per day complimenting their products and then invite readers to play along. Results vary, but I've received coupons of high-value or for free items for a number of products. I take the time to do this especially for products I rarely see coupons for but to which we are brand-loyal. For instance, my

12-year-old cat will *only* eat Purina ONE cat food. (Yes, a brand-loyal cat!) I rarely see coupons for Purina ONE cat food in my local paper, so I emailed Purina, mentioned that my cat has been eating its brand for her whole life, and thanked Purina warmly for making the product she prefers. Two weeks later, I had four Purina ONE coupons in my mailbox. Another time, I wrote to SC Johnson about how well Drano worked on a clog; a week later, a coupon for free Drano arrived. Companies will often send out coupons to help keep happy customers loyal. And if they don't, all you've lost is an investment of a couple minutes.

Also be sure to contact a company if things go wrong. Especially in the current economic climate, businesses want to hold onto their customers—and they especially don't want you bad-mouthing them to others. They know that disgruntled customers are more likely than happy customers to tell their friends about their experiences, so companies want to keep you calm! Here's a tale from my friend Joanna: While in the process of adopting her son, she was staying in Guatemala, where she bought several packages of Huggies active diapers. As she explains, "One or both tabs of every fourth diaper entirely pulled off. I emailed Kimberly-Clark, and when I got home, there were four coupons for free packs of diapers, plus another $20 worth of coupons for other Kimberly-Clark products." This cost Kimberly-Clark a lot less than losing Joanna as a customer and having her tell all her friends about the horrible experience she had with a batch of diapers in Guatemala—and she hasn't had a problem since.

This should go without saying, but always be on the lookout for sales on your favorite name brands. When you think about stockpiling, also think about stockpiling the items your family is brand-loyal to. If there is a great sale on Diet Coke (or your own beverage of choice), don't buy just one pack that week; buy several so that you don't have to pay full price for more when you go through that pack in a week or two.

Loyalty also costs us when we remain loyal to just one store. In a week when another local store just has better deals all around, try moving out of your comfort zone and see what the other store has to offer. Visiting different stores also gives you opportunities to try different brands (and find different coupons; more on that later). Although some stores will price match (Target and Walmart among them, with certain restrictions), this can get to be a pain because you have to bring in the ad for another local store and go through it item by item in order for a store to match the pricing. Stores won't match the "instant-off," money-back, or other special deals that can really maximize your savings.

A NOTE ABOUT SPECIAL DIETS

More and more of us are trying to stretch our budget while accommodating special dietary needs. This might include feeding vegetarians and vegans in the family, keeping Kosher, or eating halal meat; it might include shopping around food allergies or sensitivities, keeping a commitment to eating organic, cooking for someone with diabetes, or sticking to a low-carb diet like Atkins or South Beach. While any special diet requires that you spend more of your disposable income on food, this doesn't mean you shouldn't save as much as possible. Here are a few strategies that will help you save on any special diet.

Start online by looking up the websites of the companies that produce the products you eat most often. Contact these companies and let them know that you appreciate their products, because they will often send coupons to satisfied customers or add you to a mailing list to be the first to find out about printable coupons. Also be sure to join one or more online communities for people with similar dietary needs. Sites and blogs for those with celiac disease, for instance, often contain recipes and suggestions for affordable alternatives to common items containing gluten, and some offer coupons to members. One great example is the Be Free For Me blog (www.befreeforme.com/blog), which will help you keep up with everything related to gluten-free diets, from making gluten- and allergen-free playdough to locating gluten-free products.

If you're trying to avoid processed foods as much as possible, shop ethnic markets for items like produce and spices. The prices here can blow away those at any grocery store, the quality and selection of produce is often much better, and buying small quantities of bulk spices as needed can save you a lot while keeping your spices fresh. This is a good tip for anyone trying to add more fresh and whole foods into their diets, so explore new stores near you and see what they may have.

Another strategy here is to try as much as possible to maximize your savings in nonfood areas (such as toiletries or paper goods) and then use those savings to purchase the particular food items you need. Think creatively about how to adjust your shopping habits around the few areas in which you just can't be flexible. Here again, it all comes down to balance: If you spend more in one area, you need to save or make more in another to make up the difference. Find the balance that's right for you and your family.

Buying Organic

As more information comes out about what's really in our food, more of us are trying to eat organic as much as possible. If this includes you, the first step is to decide where to focus your efforts. Do you want to focus specifically on avoiding the "dirty dozen" most-pesticide-contaminated fruits and vegetables (www.foodnews.org), or is it important that all of your produce be

Organic Deals and Coupons blog

organic? Is it important that all your milk be organic, or do you just want it to be hormone-free? Research your options and determine your priorities.

Then, look for coupons for organic products, which you can often print right off the manufacturer's website. Visit the manufacturers' sites of your favorite organic items to see what's available. Deal blogs often do roundups of bargains on organic products, and you can find online coupons to print for everything from Muir Glen tomatoes to Cascadian Farm cereal to Stonyfield Farm yogurt. Be sure to sign up for the Organic Deals and Coupons blog (organicdeals.blogspot.com) to stay in the know about a lot of these printable coupons as well as deals on organic products at a variety of stores each week. Also check out the Organic Grocery Deals forums (www.organicgrocerydeals.com/forums) to exchange tips and deals with other organic and environmentally conscious shoppers.

Finding Coupons for Organic Products

Buyers of organic food often despair when looking through the Sunday coupon inserts, which seem to be chock-full of coupons for processed, nonorganic items. But you do have a lot of options for finding coupons for organic products; you just have to dig a little deeper! Here are a few places to try:

- Cascadian Farm (www.cascadianfarm.com/coupons): Sign up for Cascadian Farm's mailing list to receive coupons by mail.

- HealthESavers.com (www.healthesavers.com/health esavers/coupons.aspx): Find printable coupons for "natural" brands; some coupons here are for organic items, but some are for "natural" items, so be aware of what you're printing.

- Mambo Sprouts (coupons.mambosprouts.com/online_ coupons): Print coupons for various organic, natural, and allergen-free brands. You can also sign up with Mambo Sprouts (www.mambosprouts.com/coupons/free_ coupons.php) to receive coupons in the mail three times a year, or look for booklets at outlets such as Whole Foods.

- Organic Valley Co-op (www.organicvalley.coop/coupons): Print coupons for organic milk, cheese, butter, and other products.

- Seventh Generation (www.seventhgeneration.com/coupons): Print coupons for environmentally friendly items, from diapers to household cleaners.

- Stonyfield Farm (www.stonyfield.com/coupons_offers/
  index.jsp): Stonyfield Farm not only posts coupons for its
  own products, such as YoBaby yogurt, but also on occasion
  for other companies' organic products.

- Whole Foods (www.wholefoodsmarket.com/coupons): Look
  for the monthly in-store Whole Deals booklet; there are
  always plenty, and they always contain coupons. Whole
  Foods also posts selected coupons on its website.

These online coupons change regularly, so check every month
or so to see what new offers you can find.

Coupons that may seem to be for conventional products can
sometimes work for the manufacturer's organic items as well. A
coupon for Ragu pasta sauce works equally well on the conventional and organic versions, for example—it's all Ragu pasta
sauce!

Another option is to look for local alternatives. Instead of paying for
organic produce at the grocery store, you can visit your local farmer's market and get to know a local farmer and his growing methods. Some produce
may actually be grown organically, but the small farm that grows it can't
afford to go through the Food and Drug Administration's "certified
organic" process. Consider joining a community-supported agriculture
(CSA) initiative, where you "subscribe" to support a local farm and receive
weekly baskets of seasonal produce in return. Find farmers' markets, family farms, CSAs, and co-ops near you at Local Harvest (www.localharvest.
org). Also, why not try planting your own organic garden? Freeze or can as
much as possible to help see you through the winter. Start stockpiling
organic items just as you would stockpile anything else. If you find a great

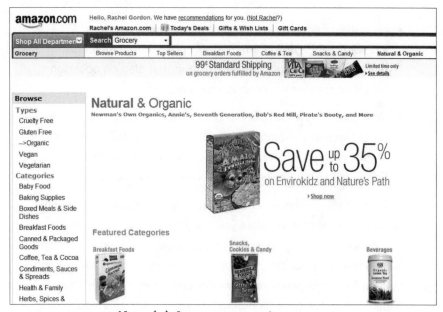

Natural & Organic section on Amazon.com

deal on organic granola bars or pasta sauce or cereal, buy more than one and store it for later.

If you don't find good options locally, or if you live in a more rural or remote location where there isn't a lot of organic competition, look online for deals. Amazon.com has an extensive organic section, for instance (and often releases discount codes or runs specials on these), and many of the manufacturers also sell direct from their own websites.

SHOP SEASONALLY

Beyond the 12-week store cycles, you can count on seasonal price cycles for many items. As I write this, for instance, school supply season is in full swing. Whether or not you have school-aged children, July and August are the best months to stock up on school and office supplies for the entire year. Are you going to need pens, notebooks, or paper in your house during the next 12 months? Buy them now at their lowest price so that you're never stuck paying full retail price. (This is also a great time to buy copy paper for your printer—because you'll need a lot of it once you start taking advantage of printable coupons!)

Once you start paying attention to store sales, these seasonal deals start making a lot of sense. The best time to buy hot dogs, paper plates, and condiments? Between Memorial Day and the Fourth of July, when everyone is having barbecues. The best time to buy cleaning supplies? Spring, when the companies are jumping on the "spring cleaning" bandwagon. The best time to buy baking supplies? November and December, when everyone is doing their holiday baking. The best time to buy a grill? At the end of the summer, when stores are closing out their displays and making room for snowblowers and other winter products. A lot of seasonal food items have a very long shelf life or freeze easily, so stock up and use them throughout the year.

Buying produce in season can save you a lot of money—and can help you try some different foods. Purchasing local in-season produce is another great way to get your family involved. Take a weekly trip to your local farmers' market, some of which feature entertainment or activities for the kids, too. Make a visit or two to a pick-your-own farm (find one near you at PickYourOwn.org). Not only does fresh fruit taste better, but it can be a lot cheaper than buying it at the store and provide a fun family experience, all in one!

Beyond the grocery store, you'll save by shopping out of season for many items. Christmas items, for instance, go as low as 90 percent off in January, so stock up on your wrapping paper, bows, tinsel, and ornaments for next year. Other good post-Christmas deals? Toys, slippers, and other popular gift items. Stock up on toys now for birthday parties throughout the year. What's nice is that deal blogs (see Chapter 3) track these types of sales and will tell you exactly when to go to Target, Walmart, or other major national retailers to cash in on these types of extreme markdowns.

If you shop for clothes out of season, you can also save substantially. Stock up on bathing suits in September, winter coats in February. This is harder to do with growing kids, when you don't know exactly what size they'll be next year, but at clearance prices, it's worth it to estimate. Leave the tags on and resell them on eBay as "new with tags" if they don't work out. Look for postholiday clearance clothing as well. Some of it isn't obviously holiday themed and can be worn year-round. I've purchased Fourth of July shorts with tiny flag logos at 90 percent off, and my older son loves the skeleton T-shirt I bought for 50 cents at 90 percent off in a Halloween clearance sale at Target.

CHANGE THE WAY YOU COOK

Just as most people shop for whatever they feel like eating in a given week, many of us tend to plan our meals around what we feel like eating in a given week or around tried-and-true family favorites. There are some really useful websites to help shake you out of that rut, find new recipes, and challenge you to lower the cost of your meals. Here are just a few of my own favorites:

- $5 dinners (www.5dollardinners.com): Posts of daily recipes for—you guessed it—dinners that cost $5 or less to make. Let the illustrated, step-by-step recipes inspire you.

- Cheap Healthy Good (cheaphealthygood.blogspot.com): This site has recipes with backstory, personality, and attitude, plus a lot of ideas on how to make expensive, complicated recipes easier and cheaper to make.

A Year of Slow Cooking

- A Year of Slow Cooking (crockpot365.blogspot.com): Save time and money by using your slow cooker. Includes recipes and illustrations galore.

Some people also swear by once-a-month cooking. Here, you basically do one full day of cooking once a month, stocking your freezer full of dinners and then pulling out meals to heat as you need them. Look at Once a Month Cooking World (www.once-a-month-cookingworld.com) for ideas. If this is too intimidating for you, try just doubling the recipe whenever you cook one of your family's favorites and freezing half to pull out on a busy

night later. This saves time and effort and reduces the chances of your turning to takeout on a busy evening.

As a first step, try to start planning a weekly menu by cooking around
the items you have stockpiled. Think: What do I currently have in the
freezer? In the pantry? And how can I just *supplement* what's already in the
house with what's on sale at the store this week?

Save and Earn to Help You Stay Home

In good economic times and in bad, a lot of us end up staying home with
our kids, giving up a full-time job to work part-time from home or to bring
in income on the side. For some of us, the work we put into strategizing our
savings is in itself a part-time job—and the more we save, the less pressure
we feel to go back to work. Others mash up their savings strategies with
various ways of making money from home to allow them to work around
their kids' schedules. In fact, 60 percent of employed mothers say they
would prefer part-time work, so if you're part of this majority, let's look for
a way to make it happen. The number one thing we're all looking for is
flexibility, so it's worthwhile to actively build flexibility into your own life.

Moms just like you are able to make this work. As Jenny S., a suburban
stay-at-home mother of two, explains, "I am a stay-at-home mom who
coupons. That is how I make my money. Without couponing I could not
stay at home and watch my kids grow. I would have to go back to work and
pay day care to do it." Some moms find that their savings strategies end up
changing their long-term goals, and they envision making couponing their
permanent part-time job. Another stay-at-home mom, Melody C., shares:

> I do see couponing as my part-time job in a way: something I
> can do to add real financial value to my family and help my
> community without compromising my goals of putting my
> energies into raising my child myself in the best way possible.

It's the most flexible part-time job I could have and is only limited by my ingenuity and effort. It also makes me feel smart and
good about myself. Staying home with young children is so
challenging, and couponing lets me use my brain and stay sharp.
I even use shopping time as alone time a couple of nights a
week, just to get out of the house without kids in tow.
Sometimes I meet up with other couponing moms, and we have
some coffee and shop together. It's a hobby that, instead of cost-
ing money, improves my family's bottom line. Couponing
means I don't have to find other ways to make money. I love the
freedom it provides. We finally feel secure because even if
something bad happened, we are stocked up on so much that we
need. We could survive for months with no income.

I'm not sure anymore that I will go back to work outside the
home. My husband and I enjoy my being CFO of our household. It gives me so much time to handle all the errands and bills
and appointments and household maintenance. It wasn't much
fun when I worked full-time. We had to use our free time to get
everything else done and had much less time to spend together.

Other moms are able to stretch out their maternity leave, take more time
at home, or move to part-time work by adjusting their spending habits.
Mother-of-two Kristine S. says, "Being able to cut the grocery/toiletries/
diaper bill down considerably has taken some pressure off of me not working. The amount I am able to save allows me to stay at home instead of
worrying about where I will get the extra few hundred I might be spending
if I weren't able to save it. I have been looking for a job just to add some
security, but in the interim, saving money through deals and couponing has
made staying at home less stressful." If you do work full-time and have less

time to strategize your trips, then start by focusing on just one store. Read a local blogger who covers your favorite store and copy her deals.

Jill Cataldo, who teaches Super-Couponing classes in the Chicago area and blogs at www.jillcataldo.com, explains:

> I absolutely see couponing as a part-time job. You can let it "engulf" you as much as you want to, but even if you don't want to spend much time on it, you can enjoy great financial savings with very little effort. The first year I couponed at this level, I saved over $5,000 with coupons. That's huge! I don't know anyone who would turn down over five grand if you handed it to them. And if you learn to cut that out of your household's budget, you've kept those thousands of dollars to spend on something else. So yes, in the way that you essentially "pay yourself" by keeping more of your money than spending it, it is a revenue source—a job.
>
> We were always committed to having at least one parent at home with our children—and I had worked as a telecommuter for over 10 years prior to starting teaching couponing. So I was already very accustomed to working at home with my children around, and they're comfortable with it, too. I work around, alongside of, and with their schedules, and the flexibility of setting your own schedule is a big benefit of working for yourself too. It always seemed counterproductive to me to pay someone to watch my children so that I could go to work; the money saver in me wanted to work from home, save on child care, and be able to earn money too. And this has allowed me to do just that.

You'll read more about Jill's couponing classes and strategies in Chapter 7. But, now that you're thinking about how to change your shopping mindset, let's move on to using online resources to find specific ways to save!

3

Get Connected Online

Now that you've started thinking about ways to change the way you shop, let's jump online and move forward with those money-saving and money-making strategies! Getting involved online is really all about *connection* and *community*. You can find literally thousands of online communities and bloggers that support both those working from home and those seeking ways to save. I want to share some of my favorites in this chapter, plus the best ways I've found to pick the ones that will be the right fit. These networks are so important in locating opportunities, saving money, sharing strategies, and shoring up your confidence. Grab the chance to get connected with other deal hunters and work-at-home moms online. When we know we're all in it together, everything just becomes a little easier.

Each blog, website, and online community has its own personality, flavor, and focus. This means that it may take a few tries to locate the right fit for you. Just as we all look for something different when choosing a neighborhood in which to live, we also all look for something different when it comes to finding the right groups or people to interact with on the internet. You might be more comfortable "lurking" in some communities but jumping right in as an active participant at others. Some communities and blogs focus on a local area or a specific type of at-home work, so following a particular local blog may make sense for you, but not as much sense for your friend across the country. Take the time to find your own comfortable online home-away-from-home.

Finding this "home" can help make the thought of saving (and earning!) money less overwhelming. As Kristine S., a mom of two, explains, "I know that I found it intimidating to think about the time commitment that might be needed to save enough money to make it worth it. Anyone who asks me about the amount I save and how I do it always seems defeated before even starting, I think because it seems like it might be a lot of work. I let them know that it is like a community. People share their experiences and deals with each other, and that helps save time. I let them know that they don't have to sit home clipping coupons, that they can get a lot of them online, and that there are a lot of coupon-matching forums and blogs which actually save you a lot of time!"

FRUGALITY AND DEAL BLOGS

Let's begin with blogs, because this is simply the easiest and best way to start finding specific ways to save money at the store. A blog is just a special sort of website that shows the most recent updates, or posts, at the top of the page, so you see the most current information easily. People started out using blogs as online journals, but now there are blogs that cover everything from politics to couponing.

These Are a Few of My Favorite Blogs ...

Here are just a few of my own favorite money-saving and frugality blogs. Get started by looking at some of these, then add in local bloggers from your own area.

- Abundant Food Savings (abundantfoodsavings.com): The thorough coverage of Safeway (Dominick's in my region) and national deals, along with coupon matchups to all the sales, helps me save!

- Baby Cheapskate (babycheapskate.blogspot.com): This is the place to go for everything baby—find deals on diapers, formula, wipes, clothes, strollers, and more!

Money Saving Mom

- It's Hip 2 Save! (hip2save.com): The blogger's goal? To show everyone, especially younger people, that saving and couponing *can* be "hip." Lots of posts, lots of deals.

- MashupMom.com (www.mashupmom.com): Yes, I'm biased. On my own blog, I talk about Chicago-area deals, national deals, online deals, and ways to make money from home.

- Money Saving Mom (www.moneysavingmom.com): Money Saving Mom is the go-to place for deals, coupons, freebies, and information on doing it right. Even though this blogger's local stores aren't the same as mine, her thorough coverage of national deals makes Money Saving Mom a must-read.

We'll each have our own list of favorites, and yours will probably change over time as your needs and priorities change and as bloggers come and go.

These are so popular because they let bloggers post, or write, new content very easily. Behind the scenes, bloggers are able to simply type into what looks like a mini word processor window and then "post" their work online with the click of a button. They don't have to know how to program or write webpages or do anything else special to get their words out there. Lots of people are now able to share their thoughts online, which means that you have literally hundreds of frugality and money-saving blogs to choose from. When you're trying to figure out which might be the best ones for you, here are some things to consider:

- Is a blogger in your local area? Most deal bloggers tend to focus more heavily on deals at their local stores, so you'll want to identify the best bloggers for the specific stores where you shop. In some places, especially in larger cities, you'll have several great blogs to choose from. Choose the one—or a couple—that's the most thorough or whose focus best matches your needs.

- How often do they update? You want to follow bloggers who update their sites on a daily basis so that you don't miss any of the deals.

Begin locating your local deal blogs at BargainBriana's Frugal Map (thefrugalmap.bargainbriana.com), as well as at The Grocery Gathering, hosted by BeCentsAble (go to www.becentsable.net and click on Store Deals). As I mentioned in Chapter 2, The Grocery Gathering rounds up various bloggers' posts about current deals at grocery stores around the country. Chrissy, co-founder (with her partner Kristin) of BeCentsAble, explains how the blog and The Grocery Gathering work: "We were two stay-at-home moms who learned to cut our budget. I was spending $800 a month on my household budget (food, personal care items, baby needs, cleaners, dog food, etc.) and now only spend $350 a month. We knew we couldn't keep this a secret! The Grocery Gathering is a resource of blogs that helps readers find deals in their areas. These are people who know these stores inside and out because this is where they shop!"

In addition to local deals, most of these blogs include online deals plus deals at nationwide chains, so you can expand your reading from the blogs that cover your area to some nonlocal blogs that best cover the other deals you need. If you find a blogger who covers Walgreens or Target or Amazon.com deals really well, for instance, you might just scroll quickly past her posts about her local grocery stores and only read the ones that pertain to you.

So how do you find more blogs to choose from? One way is by exploring the *blogroll*, or a list of other blogs, on a blog you already enjoy. Many bloggers include links to some of the blogs *they* follow in sidebars under headings such as Blogroll, My Favorite Blogs, Blogs I Read, Links, and so on. This lets their readers check out more resources that they might find useful. Others link to other bloggers in their posts; they'll give credit to another blogger for finding a deal or point out an especially useful post they saw elsewhere. Take some time to click through on these links and explore other blogs, and you'll soon find that you have more than enough places to read.

In Her Own Words

Jaime co-blogs with her husband on their money-saving website, Engineer a Debt Free Life (www. engineeradebtfreelife.com).

My husband is an engineer and came up with the name Engineer a Debt Free Life. We use our creativity and research skills to save money, make money online, and get out of debt! We help others do the same through our blog. My husband started the site in April 2008, and I started blogging there in September 2008, after I quit my job to stay at home with our son. As of early August 2009, we had about 2,200 subscribers and over 50,000 unique visitors a month.

Since we live in a small town/rural area, couponing is not very practical here since there are no "big city" stores that offer coupon deals. So we focus on money-making strategies and finding deals online. We offer proven ways to make money online, such as taking surveys and getting paid to search online. We "prescreen" the sites we post on our blog and only recommend legitimate money-making sites. We have quite a few readers who make money by doing surveys and other offers we mention on our site.

I have been surprised at how much money you can actually save by *not* working outside the home. You have more time to devote to finding freebies and deals—I had no idea some of these freebies and bargains existed [until] I quit working in 2008. It is also possible to make some money doing online surveys and by getting paid to search online—and by referring your friends to these sites. This money adds up over time and provides for lots of little "extras" we might not otherwise have! If you're just getting started, read lots of money-saving blogs. You will find great advice and ways to save money.

Many of these money-saving blogs also talk about ways to make money on the side. Some do this quite a bit, while others include only the occasional post (I run a regular "Work-at-home Saturday" feature over at MashupMom.com). These types of posts help you mash up your strategies and find ways to make it work.

MAKE INFO COME TO YOU

You don't only want to save money—you also want to save *time!* The more efficiently you can figure out the deals you want, the more time you'll have to actually take advantage of them at the store. Having to constantly remember to come back to these blogs to see what new information has been added can get crazy, especially when you start following more than one or two.

Luckily, most blogs offer an easy way to get daily updates by email. Look for an email "subscribe" form in the sidebar of your favorite blogs

"Work-at-home Saturday" on MashupMom.com

and just put in your email address (and sometimes your name) to sign up. The blog will then usually send a confirmation email message with a link that you have to click on to activate your subscription. This ensures you actually do want to receive it, so be sure to click on that link when you receive the confirmation email. These email updates usually include everything that has been posted within the past 24 hours in one long daily message, which means you only have to check your email every morning to read these updates and see what new deals are out there. (Make sure that these messages aren't getting caught in your "junk mail" filters, which can happen sometimes with email newsletters. If you see your deal blogs showing up in your junk mailbox, you can add the email addresses to your

Email subscribe form from MashupMom.com

From: noreply+feedproxy@google.com on behalf of Mashup Mom [rachel@mashupmom.com]
To:
Cc:
Subject: Mashup Mom

Mashup Mom

- **Printable coupon roundup, 8/28/09**
- **L'Oreal mascara freebie**
- **Fruitabu freebie**
- **Books a Million free shipping and clearance**
- **Super-Couponing Picnic**
- **Last Kmart doubles til 2010?**
- **The Cheesecake Factory Drive Out Hunger Tour**
- **Do your savings strategies help you get out of debt?**
- **Freebies on Friday, 8/28/09**
- **Free Chocolate Friday, 8/28/09**

Printable coupon roundup, 8/28/09

Posted: 28 Aug 2009 07:37 PM PDT

But wait, there's more! ☻

- **BOGO entree at TGIF.**

- **$2.00 off new baby Aquaphor gentle wash & shampoo.** Print **in IE** or print **in Firefox.**

- **30% off the list price of one item at Borders.** Requires (free) membership.

MashupMom.com daily email update

"approved sender" list to make sure that your email program always lets the messages through.)

Email updates work really well when you're following just a few blogs; you don't want your inbox to fill up with so many deals that other critical email gets lost. Many people solve this problem by setting up a special email account that they use just for things such as subscribing to deal blogs. This keeps those emails all in one handy place, but be sure to remember to check in each day to see what's new.

You can also subscribe to the newsfeed, or Real Simple Syndication (RSS) feed, of a particular site. RSS feeds allow you to read all the sites you have subscribed to in one place online, so that you don't have to remember to keep going back to see if something new has been posted.

 ## Using RSS Feeds

Using RSS feeds may sound technical, but it's really not all that bad! RSS is what lets you add blogs or other frequently updated sites to places such as your My Yahoo! page. You can also add these *feeds* to a special site called a *newsreader*, which brings all of the blogs you subscribe to together in one handy place. Your newsreader will show you your whole list of blogs, tell you which blogs have new posts (and how many), and let you read all of those posts right there, inside the newsreader, without having to visit each blog. This lets you easily scan through the whole list of blogs you subscribe to, instead of having to remember to go back to each site every day to see if there are any new posts. If you start following a bunch of blogs, this is the easiest way to keep track of them all.

Subscriptions list on Google Reader

First you'll need to sign up for an online newsreader account. The easiest to use is Bloglines (www.bloglines.com), and Google has a popular newsreader called Google Reader (www. google.com/reader). Once you have an account set up at one of these sites, you can start adding the blogs you read. Then just visit Bloglines or Google Reader to see what's new with all your subscriptions.

How do you know whether the blogs you want to read have these RSS feeds? Unfortunately, there is no one standard way, but here are a few:

1. Look for a little orange button on the blog. Click this to get the feed address to add to your newsreader.

2. Look for a link that says something like "Entries RSS." This will give you the feed address for the blog posts or entries.

3. Look for a link that says something like "Subscribe" or "Add RSS feed."

4. Look for a little collection of icons for popular newsreaders such as Google Reader and Bloglines. Click on the icon for your newsreader to sign up.

   For more on how to add feeds, consult the Help section in the newsreader you choose.

Another useful way to organize your list of blogs and other deal sites, especially if you're checking for deals in several places, is to use a bookmarking website like Delicious (www.delicious.com). I love Delicious because I use both a desktop computer in my office and a laptop computer when I'm in different places around the house and when I travel. I often made the mistake of bookmarking a site at home and then was unable to find or remember it when on the road—which got pretty frustrating after a while! Delicious is so useful because it lets you store your bookmarks right on the internet so that you can get to them from anywhere you happen to be—at home, at the library, at a friend's house, or anywhere else. Just create an account and then add and organize your bookmarks by keywords to help you easily find them later.

FRUGALITY SITES AND NEWSLETTERS

Beyond blogs, you can check out other types of frugality sites, as well as online money-saving and deal newsletters. Some of these sites also contain blogs within them, just to make things confusing. Here are a few to start with:

- The Dollar Stretcher (www.stretcher.com): As its tagline (Living Better … for Less) suggests, the Dollar Stretcher focuses on ways to save—on *everything*. Sign up for its email newsletters to get regular updates. In its associated forums, community members discuss everything from frugal cooking to debt management.

- Frugal Village (www.frugalvillage.com): The Frugal Village community has everything from articles to forums to tips to printable coupons—everything you might want to know about frugal living and others to share your ideas with.

- Wise Bread (www.wisebread.com): This catch-all site contains forums, articles, blogs, and more, all about "living large on a small budget." Find everything from frugality tips to bargains to personal finance advice.

You'll also find links to other frugality sites from the frugality blogs you follow, so take some time to see which, if any, might be right for you.

BARGAIN-HUNTING EMAIL GROUPS

Some people just prefer email. Luckily, there are bargain-hunting groups on Yahoo! where members sign up to exchange email messages about local deals. For instance, the group Chicago Area Bargain Hunting Parents (groups.yahoo.com/group/Chicago_bargain_hunting_moms) focuses on— you guessed it—deals in the Greater Chicago area; the group Southeast Louisiana Bargains (finance.groups.yahoo.com/group/SoutheastLouisiana Bargains) targets deals in the Baton Rouge, New Orleans, and southern Louisiana area. When you sign up for one of these groups, you receive every message other members post right in your email box, and they all receive everything you email back.

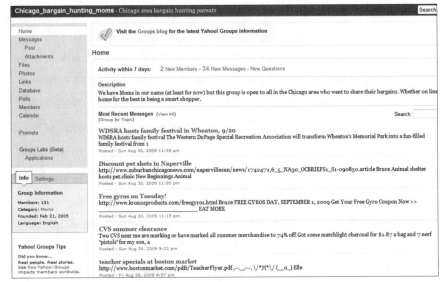

Chicago Area Bargain Hunting Parents

Deal Forums

Moving on to deal forums can be kind of a big step for many people. Online communities focused on finding the best deals range from small local groups to bustling national forums. Some are more welcoming than others to *newbies*, or new users, so take the time to find a comfortable fit. You might find it helpful to lurk for a while, just watching the action and getting a feel for the types and pace of conversations before jumping in yourself. Once you get the hang of how forums run, though, be sure to pick one as your home site and to post about any deals you find. These communities work because they bring together the brainpower of hundreds—or even thousands—of members. You might spy one deal, while someone six towns over might spy another (or 10!). But when you both share what you find with the group, everyone benefits.

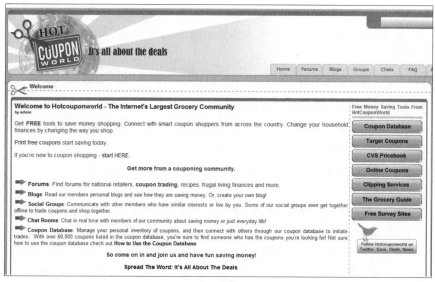

Hot Coupon World

The major national deal forums include:

- A Full Cup (www.afullcup.com)

- Hot Coupon World (www.hotcouponworld.com)

- Slickdeals (www.slickdeals.net)

Some smaller forums can be more welcoming to new members and slightly less overwhelming. These, though, may have fewer deals for some stores because not as many people are participating in finding and figuring them out. Smaller forums tend to be heavier on deals at one or two stores where members tend to congregate. Among these, Vicky's Deals (www.vickysdeals.com) is one of my own favorites. Again, take your time to find the best fit for you. Look at the coverage of your local stores and favorite chains. See how active a given forum is, whether it covers the deals at stores you shop at, and how welcoming the members are.

WORK-AT-HOME SITES AND COMMUNITIES

If you're working at home, it's really easy to start feeling isolated after a while. Trust me, I know! Having limited contact with other adults isn't healthy for anyone. While getting out to talk to people in person is best, connecting with others online can also help you feel more motivated and hooked into the grown-up world.

Online forums are also some of the best places to get honest feedback on what certain types of at-home work are like and which companies are on the up-and-up. Always do your research before you start. Carly R., an Ohio mother of one who scores tests for the Educational Testing Service and does online tutoring for Brainfuse, says that when you're looking for work-at-home opportunities, "Don't get discouraged. I have had a ton of things that haven't worked out for me. … It takes time and patience, plus some failures, to find the best things that work for you and your family. I also would recommend doing your research. Check out some work-at-home message boards, join, and ask questions. Most of the time you can get answers before committing to a particular project. There are legitimate [work-at-home] opportunities, but don't jump into things too quickly."

Here are just a few sites and communities to get you started:

- Home-Based Working Moms (www.hbwm.com): This online community contains everything from forums to blogs to articles and resources.

- Sparkplugging (www.sparkplugging.com): This site bills itself as containing work-at-home resources and community for "Web 2.0 entrepreneurs" but includes other work-at-home info as well.

Blog posts and other info often focus on using the internet to market a home business and otherwise use online resources.

- WAHM.com (www.wahm.com): This site has an active forum of work-at-home moms, as well as an active job postings board with work-at-home and freelance opportunities.

- *Why* Magazine (www.workhomeyou.com): This online magazine includes short, to-the-point articles on common questions, pitfalls, and perks of working at home.

- Work-at-Home Success (workathomesuccess.com): Find information, resources, and reviews about various work-at-home opportunities.

- Work Place Like Home (www.workplacelikehome.com): You'll need to register before you can read the forums here, but this busy online community offers everything from support to advice to work-at-home job listings.

Be careful to avoid work-at-home scams. Any site that offers you guaranteed income or ways to get rich quick isn't likely to be legitimate. Beyond these general sites, you'll also want to look into sites and forums aimed specifically at people who do the particular kind of at-home work you do (or would like to do), because their community and resources will probably better fit your needs.

Social Networking Sites

You have probably used, or at least heard of, sites such as MySpace and Facebook to keep in touch with friends. But did you know that companies also use these types of sites? These companies know that many of the people they want to reach spend a lot of time on places like Facebook and Twitter, so they see social networking sites as a great way to get in touch with consumers—that's you! For this reason, companies have jumped on the social networking bandwagon. Usually, they ask people to "follow," "fan," or "friend" them on these sites—which gets their info in front of you when you log in, just as your real friends' news shows up. The companies hold out the potential of coupons, discounts, or other offers as enticements to encourage you to follow them. Would you friend or fan a restaurant for a free appetizer or a company for a great discount? They surely hope so! (Remember, you can always "unfriend" or "unfan" them later.) Companies walk a fine line here, though, as people primarily use these sites to connect with friends and tend to resist heavy-handed attempts at marketing and corporate speak.

The two social networks that companies hang out on most often are Facebook and Twitter. If you're not yet on these sites, you might think about setting up an account to connect with friends, companies, and other deal seekers. Frugal bloggers also spend time and ask people to friend or follow them on these sites, giving you another way to find out about deals in a timely fashion. Look in the sidebars or About pages of your favorite blogs to see whether they have information about how to follow them on Twitter or Facebook as well.

How do these sites work? Twitter is what's known as a *microblogging* site, where people have 140 characters or less to post each of their thoughts and comments. Their friends follow them on Twitter to keep up with what they're doing and thinking. Companies have jumped onto Twitter because they know that consumers use the site all day long to keep in touch with friends and other people they subscribe to, or follow. In fact, Twitter had almost 23 million unique visitors in December 2009 alone! Try following your own favorite companies on Twitter because you never know what they might post, from coupon offers to one-day-only special deals. Find Twitter overwhelming? Start with CheapTweet (cheaptweet.com or twitter.com/cheaptweet), which scans Twitter for the best sales, coupons, and deals

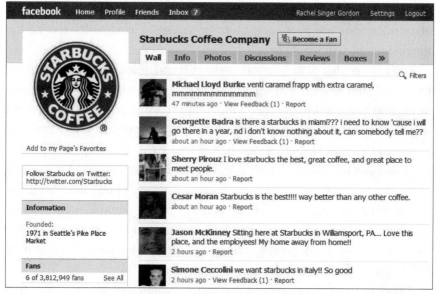

Starbucks page on Facebook

everyone else is talking about. The deals that the most people are discussing rise to the top, so you can find hot bargains instantly.

Facebook is a more diverse social networking site and is even more popular—it had 134 million visitors in January 2010. Beyond allowing people
to make short "status update" posts that show up on their friends' pages,
Facebook also allows individuals and companies to create pages on the
site. Other Facebook users can become a "fan" of those pages and follow
companies or other users on Facebook. When you become a fan of your
favorite companies or products on Facebook, you never know what might
be in store! Savvy companies regularly reward their loyal customers—that
is, people who have taken the time to become their fans—with coupons,
sweepstakes, games, or other opportunities. Companies and products from
Caribou Coffee to Oreos to Stacy's Pita Chips to Starbucks Coffee have

offered free product coupons to fans on Facebook, and these sorts of offers and promotions are becoming more prevalent as companies realize the importance of social networks.

You can see that getting online is the best and quickest way to get in the know and start saving. You want to be one of the first ones to know about deals, and you want to connect with companies and bloggers to get these ongoing offers and discounts. Helen T., a self-described newlywed and cat mom who enjoys saving money in her free time, sums up what online resources can do: "While I have always been a smart shopper, I learned all about the online savings community about a year ago and have been 'on fire' ever since. This has definitely come in handy with pay cuts coupled with rising prices in the stores. While I wouldn't say the economic down-turn has led me to couponing, I'd say the ramped-up savings that started before the economy tanked have only helped me."

Ramp up your own savings by getting connected online. Now that you're hooked in to some ways to find discounts and online communities, let's move on to some specific ways to save at the store.

4

Get in the Game

Now that you're connected, it's time to get in the savings game! Why do I call it a game? Because once you get into doing these deals, it *does* become almost like a game. In fact, there's even the site I mentioned in Chapter 2, the Grocery Game (www.thegrocerygame.com), which matches up coupons, sales, and deals for just about every store imaginable. But I suggest paying for this subscription site only if you need a kick start or have a serious lack of time, as you'll be paying for the convenience of packaged info that is readily available elsewhere online. (The Grocery Game does offer a free 4-week trial so you can see how the site works and whether it's right for you.)

I have so much fun playing the savings game and seeing how much I can save at the store—and I know you will, too! Even my 7-year-old gets a kick out of watching the numbers go down at the register and trying to guess how much the final total will turn out to be. This is one way to get your family into saving and to get your kids into good habits that will serve them well for life. Seeing how much you save, beyond being incredibly useful in tough economic times, is just downright fun. Trying to beat your personal best, or getting a "high" from putting together the best possible deal, is itself the best antidote to any sense of deprivation from the adjustment to living frugally.

So let me tell you what I've learned about getting in the game. I'll tell you how to find the best deals at your local grocery and drugstores and how to buy everyday items for pennies on the dollar. You'll find out how to do everything from printing coupons to finding sales to loading electronic coupons onto your store loyalty cards. You'll discover the best ways to use coupons and mash up strategies to maximize your savings—and you'll learn why changing the way you shop is the necessary first step.

The most important thing I've learned on my couponing journey? Don't try right off the bat to imitate the stories you see on TV. You know the ones: those news and talk show clips where "coupon queens" easily walk into a random store and scoop up hundreds of dollars worth of groceries for just pennies. That's both unrealistic and frustrating for most people. While such trips are occasionally *possible*, they're not the *norm*, so these types of stories just set you up for frustration. Comparing your shopping trip to a trip staged for TV can make you believe that couponing is something you'll never "get" or that it's a waste of your time.

What you *can* do is solidly (and easily) save a good 30 percent to 50 percent—or more—on your monthly grocery bill. What you *can* do is get most of your toiletries and much of your over-the-counter medication for pennies or for free—imagine never having to pay for toothpaste again! What you *can* do is start small, then build your savings higher each week as you get more comfortable with the process and build up your stockpile of staples and coupons. What you *can* do is combine strategies, add up the savings, and mash up your own path to success. What you *can* do is build your way up to the occasional TV-camera-worthy trip. Start by figuring out how to "do the deals" at just one store and then move up from there.

Following are some of my favorite strategies to help get you started on your own path to saving.

SAVE ON GROCERIES

Now that you're ready to change your shopping approach, get started by saving on groceries each week. This is one of the most important changes you can make: The cost of food has been skyrocketing, just as we need to be saving, and manufacturers have been reducing the sizes of their items, when they're not busy raising prices. That means that you get less for your money, right when you need to be getting more! So get ready to fight back. Let's start with a few of the simplest ways to start saving—again, being sure to check your store ads for current sales and deals each week before you shop.

Shop loss leaders. Loss leaders are those few items that go on sale each week for tremendous savings: 99-cent cereal, or 10-cent apples, or $1 boxes of granola bars. Stores bank on the fact that people are lazy—or at least busy! Once they get us in the door with the promise of a great deal on a few items, we're likely to just do *all* of our shopping at that store. That lets them easily make their money back, and then some, on their higher-priced items. Tell yourself that it's OK to walk out with just the loss leaders, to "cherry-pick" the best deals and move on. Most people think that chasing the deals isn't worth it, but studies have actually shown that "cherry pickers" save more money by doing this than it costs them in time—and that they save even more if they buy a lot of each extreme deal item and then stockpile it for later.

If you have several stores near you, try to plan one big shopping trip each week (without kids, if possible). Make a little circle to hit more than one store and grab just the best deals at each, because this alone can mean significant savings. If your store is out of a loss leader, ask for a rain check at the customer service counter so that you can get it for the sale price at a later date. Stores sometimes like to play games themselves by only stock-ing a limited supply of an advertised loss leader. Remember, they are think-ing that once they get you in, you're likely to just stay and shop even if the "deal" is already gone. Always, always grab that rain check so you can get the loss leader at your convenience later.

Shop clearance items. This includes clearance meat and dairy, as long as you use or freeze it by its expiration date. Get to know when your local stores mark down perishables that are close to their expiration dates. I know that my local Dominick's, for instance, has fantastic meat clearance deals early each morning. So if I go in at 7AM, I can often get meat at 30 percent to 50 per-cent off. If you do this often, you might want to invest in an extra freezer!

Only buy things that are on sale. "Regular" grocery and drugstore prices on most items are ridiculously high, but a good chunk of the store will be on sale in any given week. Remember those 12-week sales cycles? This is where you want to take advantage of them. Take a few minutes to browse your local stores' ads each week and pick out the best deals. Structure your shopping list and your week's menus around these deals and what you have in your stockpile. If you can, also spend some time walking around the store because you'll often find unadvertised sales and deals. Companies often pay to have their products featured in grocery ads, whether or not they're actually on "sale." And remember: Just because it's in the ad, doesn't mean it's a good deal. The store can *say* something is on sale— even if the sale price is just a few cents below its normal insanely high shelf price—but that doesn't necessarily mean the price has hit its 12-week low or that it's even a good price.

Believe it or not, the *deals* are often better at stores that tend to have higher *everyday* prices. People think they'll always save money shopping at Aldi or Sam's Club or Super Walmart. You will, if you just compare your *everyday* savings there to the normal shelf prices at midrange grocery stores. However, if you make a habit of shopping *only* the loss leaders, sale items, and money-back items (we'll talk about these in a bit) at "regular" grocery stores, you can actually do much, much better.

Know how to read your ads. Stores often advertise sales such as "10 for $10." Unless it says you *must* buy 10 to get that pricing, you can buy just one item for $1. Another trick: Stores advertise sales such as "buy 2, get 2 free." What they generally do here is raise the price on the two you have to buy so that it's not actually much of a deal, but it sounds like you're getting a great bargain. One of my local stores, for instance, does this with 12-packs of soda once a month or so. Its normal, nonsale price for brand-name soda is $4.50 per pack. When it does a "buy 2, get 2 free" promotion, it will temporarily raise that price to $6.50 per pack so that you *really* pay $13 for four, or $3.25 per pack. This is a sale, true, but it doesn't save you anywhere near as much as "buy 2, get 2 free" would if it were based on the usual nonsale price—and it's not actually a great price for soda. The local deal blogs you follow will keep you in the know when something really is a good sale price.

Match sales to coupons. You save so much more by matching your coupons to items that are on sale because when you do this, you *save twice on the same item.* Watch for any opportunity to layer on more than one kind of savings. This can be especially useful in areas of the country where stores double manufacturer coupons up to a certain amount. (My hometown unfortunately isn't one of them!)

Shop the perimeter of the store. Make a circle around the inner aisles because the outside aisles generally contain "whole" foods: produce, meat, and dairy. Whole foods, aside from being better for you in general, cost much less than processed foods. If you don't have as much time to coupon or to plan as you'd like, just remember this: A bag of potatoes will set you back a lot less for the same amount of food than a bunch of boxes of processed potato side dishes. Fresh chicken breast will cost you less than prepackaged, precooked chicken strips. And a loaf of bread and a pack of deli meat will cost you less than a premade deli sandwich.

Compare apples to apples. Think about "per unit" costs (per hundred, per pound, per quart, etc.), especially in this age of the incredible shrinking product. When companies change their packaging, which they've been doing a lot lately, this is sometimes to hide the fact that the contents have been reduced. Compare the package sizes of cereal, ice cream, diapers, and even cheese over the past few years. Each is getting smaller while the price is staying the same or even increasing. When one brand shrinks, another brand might then become a better value (until that brand also shrinks). When you are deciding which brand of, let's say, yogurt cups to buy, realize that one brand's cups might be 6 oz. whereas another's might be 4 oz.— that's a pretty serious difference. When you are deciding which brand of cheese to buy, realize that some brands are now 7 oz. instead of 8 oz. This doesn't sound too bad, but it's really a 12.5 percent difference. (If you had a coupon for 12.5 percent off a bag of shredded cheese, you'd use it, right?) What this means is that you are *paying 12.5 percent more*—not to mention, a 12.5 percent difference can mess up your recipes if you're not paying attention! So always look at how much you are paying *per unit* (per diaper, per ounce, per liter). This information is usually printed on the shelf tags right under the product price.

Realize that bigger is not always better. We've become so trained to believe that the best deals come from buying in bulk that we often overlook the deals that are right in front of our noses. Again, look at that *per unit* price. Stores often put smaller sizes on sale, making them the better buy than their bigger counterparts. Using coupons on cheaper, smaller items also saves you *more.* Saving $1 off a $1.50 item is a much better deal than saving $1 off a $5 item: It saves you more per unit and a bigger percentage of the sale price.

Watch out for tricks that offer convenience over price. One thing that really drives me crazy? Those newer juices that are mixed 50/50 with water. These are billed as letting you pour juice for your toddler right out of the bottle rather than mixing it with water from your own tap. Does this juice cost half as much at the store? Of course not! It costs the same as a bottle of 100 percent juice—*but it lasts half as long* as a regular bottle you mix with water. How much are the few seconds it takes to add water to a cup of juice worth? Another example is the 100-calorie pack. You're paying a lot extra here for the convenience of prepackaging. If you need to limit portions, buy a bag of chips or pretzels or cookies or crackers and repackage it yourself into individual baggies as soon as you get home from the store. Not only will you save money, but you will often be able to get a better-quality product when you don't limit yourself to what happens to be available in 100-calorie portions.

Companies count on consumers to just shop the way they're used to, tossing products into the cart because they are familiar with the brand or like the packaging or fall for the advertising. Savvy shoppers save on each trip just by paying a bit more attention at the store.

DRUGSTORE SAVINGS

Saving at the drugstore works a lot like saving at the grocery store. When it comes to drugstore savings, though, your best bet will be to stick to the biggest three chains: CVS, Walgreens, and Rite Aid. I will talk more about CVS and Walgreens here because I'm more familiar with their deals, but you can find out more about how Rite Aid works via the Drugstore section at "Cents"able Momma (www.centsablemomma.com). Drugstores are where you'll start getting yourself those *free*—yes, I said *free*—toiletries on a regular basis. You don't normally want to buy these types of items at the grocery store, because you'll often find much better deals at drugstores. How?

Shop the loss leaders. Sound familiar? Do this just the same way you would at the grocery store. While grocery stores usually advertise food items as loss leaders, drugstores often do the same sort of thing with toiletries, letting you grab super-cheap shampoo, toothpaste, deodorant, and so on for your stockpile. Wait for these sales to buy what you need. Everyday prices at drugstores are high, but their advertised loss leaders each week aim to get people in the door. Walgreens, for example, may offer a given brand of deodorant for 99 cents one week with an in-ad coupon, which you can combine with a dollar-off manufacturer's coupon from the newspaper to get yourself some free deodorant. CVS might offer hair dye at a free-after-coupon price the next week. This is another reason to stockpile commonly used items—buy them during these mega sales and you'll never have to buy them at regular price.

Shop clearance items. This is especially fun at drugstores when you shop seasonally. For instance, they tend to stock a lot of toys, wrapping paper, and gift items before Christmas. After the holiday, they want those things off the shelves as fast as possible to make room for the next set of seasonal deals because their space is much more limited than at grocery or big box stores.

Match sale items to coupons. Drugstores often provide their own store coupons for items they're already discounting. Walgreens includes coupons in its in-store flyer every week, and CVS lets you scan your loyalty card at its in-store price scanner to print out coupons at each visit.

Shop money-back items. Each drugstore chain also has a money-back or rebate program. These programs allow you to get money back on everyday purchases, and the money-back deals are advertised in each store's weekly flyer. Use these programs wisely by *only* buying the money-back products each week, and then "rolling" the money you get back into new money-back items. This can get a little bit confusing, but it is simply the best way to save at these stores. Here's how it works.

CVS has a program called Extra (Care) Bucks (ECB). ECB can be used like cash toward your next in-store purchase, and they are printed out right on your receipt when you buy an eligible item using your CVS (ExtraCare) card. The CVS weekly ad lists which items will be earning ECB that week. The trick here? Match your coupons to items that are already giving you money back! For instance, let's say that CVS has Colgate toothpaste on sale this week for $2.99, but you will also get back $2 in ECB when you buy a tube. You have a $1-off coupon for Colgate toothpaste. Use your coupon to buy that tube of toothpaste, spend $1.99, and get $2 back. You essentially got your Colgate for free! (Realize that CVS often limits the number of times you can do these deals per card, generally between one and five, and that these limits are listed in the ads.)

Even better: Now take that $2 you just earned, and look at the ad again to see what other items will earn you ECB this week. You might see that you can buy shampoo on sale for $3.50 and get $1 in ECB back—but you also have a $1-off manufacturer coupon from the paper, *and* you now have $2 in ECB from the toothpaste purchase. You will now spend just 50 cents on the shampoo (your $3.50 sale price, minus the $2 in ECB you already have and the $1 coupon), and you will get another $1 in ECB back. Now you've only spent $2.49 (plus tax) on shampoo *and* toothpaste, and you still have $1 in ECB left to play the game again or hold on to for next week's deals.

CVS also releases "dollars off" your next purchase coupons fairly often, either at the in-store scanner or via email. (Be sure to register your card at cvs.com and check the option for email alerts in order to receive these random printable coupons in your inbox.) For example, if you have a "$4 off a $20 purchase" CVS coupon, you can use that *first* on a $20 purchase before applying any of your other coupons or ECB. This can translate into significant savings.

Walgreens has a similar program called Register Rewards (RR). Unlike CVS, Walgreens doesn't currently have limits on the number of times you can do an RR deal each week. However, you can't use the RR you earn on one item to buy that same item again and earn more RR. You can, however, use RR to buy something *else* that gets you more RR. For example, let's say our tube of Colgate toothpaste is on sale at Walgreens for $2.99 with $2 in RR back. If you try to use that $2 in RR to buy another tube of Colgate toothpaste, you won't get another $2 in RR. But, let's say that you buy shampoo using those $2 in RR and earn a new $1 in RR on that shampoo. Now, you can use that $1 in RR from the shampoo to buy toothpaste again, earning another $2 in RR. You can keep going back and forth between toothpaste and shampoo (or other items), as long as you use your RR to purchase a different product each time.

Another strange quirk at Walgreens: RR are counted as *manufacturer coupons*, and the number of manufacturer coupons you use at Walgreens cannot exceed the number of items you are buying; the last one will beep at the register and will not scan. So let's say you have a $3 RR, and you want to buy a $4 item using that RR but you also want to use a $1 coupon for that item—you can't do it! The registers will "see" you as using two manufacturer coupons for the same product, which just isn't allowed. Here's what to do: Add something small in your order (a pencil or a caramel) to make the number of manufacturer coupons come out even with (or less than) the number of items.

All this may seem confusing when you first read about it, but it begins to make more sense as you start to do it at the store and see how it works. When you're reading those deal blogs, you'll see that most of them walk you through the best CVS, Walgreens, or Rite Aid deals each week. Simply copy some of their ideas until you get the hang of figuring them out on your own. You'll read more later in this chapter about Catalina deals at the grocery store, which work much the same way.

STACK AND SAVE

Now let's get a little more advanced! Because you've learned some of the basic strategies for saving at the grocery and drugstore, it's time to start adding in coupon savings and combining methods together for some *real* savings. Here's what's most important to remember: Saving one time on one item is good. Saving two or more times on that same item is much, *much* better. So what does it mean to "stack" your savings at the store? *Stacking* just means that you are saving in more than one way on a single item, or "stacking up" your savings. The more ways you can save, the better. Let's talk first about some different ways to save, then about how to mash them up for maximum savings.

Look for electronic coupons that you can load right onto your store loyalty card. On these electronic coupon (ecoupon) sites, you generally log in and enter the number printed on the back of your store card. You can add the coupons you like best from a list of available discounts, or depending on the site, the coupons may just load onto your card automatically once you view the page. Discounts on these items will automatically come off at the register when you use your card to purchase the qualifying items.

 ## Finding and Loading Ecoupons

Here are a few places you can find and load ecoupons:

- Avenu at Jewel-Osco (avenu.jewelosco.com/groceries/ EntryPage), Albertson's (www.albertsons.com/avenusc/ avenu-home.html), and other Albertson's or SuperValu chain stores: To use Avenu, you need to log into the Avenu section of your local store's website. There, you'll simply punch in the number on the back of your store loyalty card to view and activate these special savings, which change on a regular basis. Simply view the list of ecoupons to activate them, and the discounts come off automatically at the register when you purchase any of the qualifying items.

- Cellfire (www.cellfire.com): This program also loads coupons right onto your store loyalty card, but you need to "add" the individual coupons you want from a list of available discounts. Participating chains include Kroger, Shoprite, and Safeway (which includes stores such as Safeway, Dominick's, Genuardi's, Randall's, Tom Thumb, and Vons), and discounts come off automatically at the register.

- P&G eSaver (www.pgesaver.com): Safeway stores partner with P&G (Procter & Gamble) on an eSaver program that allows you to load P&G coupons right onto your store loyalty card from this website. Again here, you need to choose the coupons you want in order to activate them.

- Shortcuts (www.shortcuts.com): Safeway and Kroger stores participate in the Shortcuts program. Log in to Shortcuts and enter your store loyalty card number to see what coupons might be available. Click "Add" on each ecoupon you want to load onto your card.

- Zavers (www.zavers.com/home): Stores participating in the Zavers program include A&P, Waldbaum's, Superfresh, Food Emporium, Pathmark, and Cooke's. Choose the ecoupons you want to load, then click "Save It!" to add to your card.

One thing to realize here is that some store cards will only hold a certain number of coupons across all these sites. So if you load Safeway coupons at both P&G eSaver and Shortcuts, for instance, you need to be careful not to hit that limit.

Shortcuts electronic coupons

Ecoupons are convenient because you don't have to remember to clip and bring coupons with you every time you go to the store, and you don't have to worry about them not scanning. The discounts just come off automatically at the register.

Look for printable store coupons that you can bring to the store. Some stores offer printable store coupons right on their websites! Check out these sites:

- CVS (www.cvs.com and click "in-store coupons"): CVS includes store coupons and manufacturer coupons on its printable coupons site, so be sure to look at the wording to see which is which. The CVS ones will show up first in the list.

- Meijer MealBox (www.meijermealbox.com): Meijer regularly releases MealBox or store coupons on its site that can be combined with manufacturer coupons for extra savings.

- Safeway (www.safeway.com/ifl/grocery/Coupons): If you shop at another Safeway chain store such as Dominick's or Randall's, check your own store's site to find the same store and manufacturer coupons, but with your local store's logo on them. Safeway also allows you to load these coupons onto your card as ecoupons rather than printing them out. Be careful with this, however: Once you've loaded a manufacturer coupon to your Safeway card, you can no longer print it, which prevents you from later printing it to use in a different store.

- SuperTarget grocery coupons (sites.target.com/site/en/super target/page.jsp?title=coupons_specials): These coupons can also be used at regular Targets, but only SuperTargets carry all the grocery items.

Also look up the websites for your own local grocery and drugstores to see what coupons they have online or what you can sign up for. There's more about printable coupons and troubleshooting printing problems later in this chapter. Be sure to get on each store's email list, because sometimes you'll get extra coupons to print right from your email box.

Also keep an eye out for paper store coupons in your Sunday paper and in those midweek mailed ads that most people just throw away. If you don't get yours in the mail, look at the fliers at store entrances, because you can often clip coupons right out of there. Tear them out while you're shopping, or throw a small pair of scissors or a Swiss army knife into your purse so you can clip them neatly on the go.

Look for announcements of "instant" savings on particular items. Instant savings take money off the items you're buying right now when you

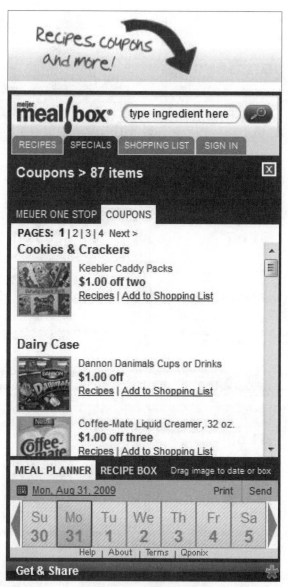

Meijer MealBox coupons

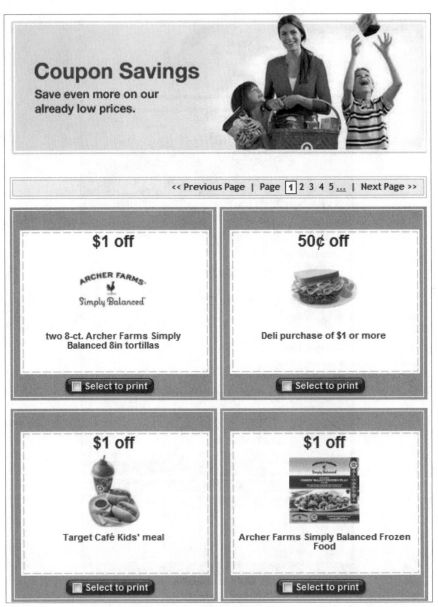

Target printable coupons

buy a particular combination or dollar amount. You'll see in-store advertisements such as "Buy 5 participating products, save $5 instantly!" Keep in mind that some store fliers show you the price of products *after* the instant savings, and some show the price *before* the instant savings. Be aware of this so that you know how much you're actually saving and how much you're going to have to pay.

Look for on-your-next-order savings on particular items. On-your-next-order savings will print out Catalinas, or coupons good toward your next purchase at that store. (Yes, this is a weird name, but Catalina is actually the name of the company that makes the machines that print these out!) Catalinas work much the same as the ECB at CVS and RR at Walgreens. You don't see the savings on this order, but you get a coupon that you can use like cash toward your next in-store purchase. One thing to remember about Catalinas: *They expire.* If you let them expire, it's like throwing away money! I'll talk more in depth about Catalinas in a bit.

Before you start playing the savings game, be sure to familiarize yourself with your local stores' coupon policies. Some will accept expired manufacturer coupons that go back anywhere from 30 days to one year; others will refuse coupons even a day after their expiration dates. Some will accept all coupons printed from the internet; some won't accept printed

Catalina coupon

coupons at all, and others will take them, but with certain limitations. Some will only double coupons up to a certain dollar amount, some never double coupons, and some run occasional double (or even triple) coupon events. If you forget to bring a coupon, some stores will allow you to bring it back with your receipt to receive the savings later. Check your store's website to see if it has a link to its coupon policy; if so, you might want to print it and bring it with you to the store in case you have any problems. If you have a problem redeeming coupons at a local store, you can email or call the corporate office for clarification and ask that an email stating the coupon policy be sent to you to keep for future reference.

Now, Stack!

Phew! That's a lot of ways to save. But now let's start mashing these different ways up to *really* score some deals. First—and this is something that will change your shopping life forever—did you know that you can stack a *manufacturer's* coupon on top of a paper or printed *store* coupon? This means that you can use two coupons on one item, in effect saving twice. This is allowed and encouraged because the funds come out of two different pots. The store is offering its coupon as a *store* discount, which is basically another way for the store to put an item on sale. The store will be reimbursed by the manufacturer for the manufacturer coupon as a *manufacturer* discount, and for its trouble, the store will also make a few extra cents on each manufacturer coupon. How do you tell the difference between a store and manufacturer coupon? A manufacturer coupon will say "manufacturer coupon" on the top and will have a mailing address in the fine print (where the retailer needs to send the coupon to for reimbursement).

So, for example, if the store has a store coupon in its weekly ad for 50 cents off a box of cereal, and you have a manufacturer coupon from the newspaper for 75 cents off the same type of cereal, go ahead and use them both. You'll get $1.25 off that one box of cereal. Not bad! If you go to Target's website and find a Target coupon for $1 off ice cream, and you also have a newspaper coupon for $1 off ice cream, use them both at Target to get $2 off that one carton of ice cream.

Remember, though, *you can never stack two paper manufacturer coupons on the same item, even if the coupons are for different amounts.* This is because the savings on both coupons come out of the same "pot," the manufacturer's pocket.

But here's where it starts to get interesting. It's not just paper coupons you can stack. You can stack additional *electronic* savings onto both your store and your manufacturer coupons. Use coupons together with the electronic savings that you have already loaded onto your store card. While these ecoupons are currently limited to just a few families of stores, they are likely to become more common as people grow more accustomed to these types of programs.

To add to the confusion, while some of these ecoupons are manufacturer coupons, they currently *can* be combined with paper manufacturer coupons for additional savings. This is the *only* time you can combine manufacturer coupons. Again, you cannot combine two paper manufacturer coupons in the same way. When you read the fine print on these ecoupon sites, you'll find that you're "discouraged" to use of these ecoupons with manufacturer coupons, but it's not forbidden. Sometimes by the end of the month, I don't even remember what I've loaded onto my card until I see electronic savings come off at the register.

Now let's start thinking about stacking those electronic and paper coupons together with sales. Let's say your favorite cereal is on sale for $1.50 per box. Not bad. But then you realize you have a 50-cents-off manufacturer coupon—even better! Then you look at your ecoupons on Avenu and find you have another 75 cents off that brand of cereal that will come off automatically at the register—now we're talking! Here, you're layering three kinds of savings together: a sale, a manufacturer coupon, and a store coupon. This makes your own out-of-pocket cost for that box of cereal just 25 cents after all is said and done. (My own final target price for most brand-name cereal, by the way, is 25 cents a box.)

Cheerios	$1.50 per box (sale price)
Avenu coupon	- .75
Manufacturer coupon	- .50
Your cost	$ .25

 Know When to Hold 'Em

When you start to use coupons to maximize your savings, one of the best tips I can give you is to hold out for the best moment to use your higher value coupons or any _free_ or _buy-one-get-one-free_ coupons you run across. Here's when to use these to get the best possible savings:

- Use a _free_ or _buy-one-get-one-free_ manufacturer coupon together with a store's buy-one-get-one-free sale. At most stores, this will get you _two_ items for free. Let me repeat: You will get _two_ items for free! Why? The store is giving you one free in its sale. You are using your coupon to purchase the other one—and the store will get paid back by the manufacturer. Net result: two free items! Remember when I mentioned that I had some _free_ laundry detergent in my stockpile? A few months ago, Purex released a limited-time buy-one-get-one-free coupon online. I printed mine right then and there and held onto them. A few weeks later, my local grocery store ran a buy-one-get-one-free sale on Purex, so I strolled in with my coupons and walked out paying only tax for my bottles of detergent. And those two free Hershey's bars that so delighted my son? Same type of deal.

- Use a *free* coupon when you can combine it with a store coupon that requires you to spend a certain dollar amount. For example: Let's say your local grocery store's weekly ad includes a coupon for $5 off a $50 purchase. You generally have to hit that $50 mark *before you use any coupons* (and before sales tax is added). So one good plan is to choose items that help you get up to $50 that you know you'll end up getting free after using a coupon. Your actual out-of-pocket cost, after coupons, will be much lower than $50. (Hand the cashier that $5-off-a-$50-purchase coupon *first*, then hand over your other coupons.)

- Use higher-value coupons in conjunction with sales in order to maximize your savings. When we get a good coupon, our impulse is to run out and use it immediately. However, if we wait for a sale, we can save even more!

- Use coupons on smaller, cheaper items. This runs counter-intuitive to our impulses: We tend to think we save more on bigger items. When we use a coupon on a smaller, lower-priced item, though, we save a bigger percentage of the sales price. It's almost always better to use a $2 coupon on a $4 item (saving 50 percent) than to use it on a $10 item (saving just 20 percent).

- Save higher-value coupons for double coupon events. Kmart, for instance, has been running regular promotions at participating stores where it doubles manufacturer coupons with a face value up to and including $2. This can make for some great deals—and makes a lot of items *free* after coupon.

  Of course, if your free, higher-value, or buy-one-get-one-free coupons are nearing their expiration dates and you haven't found a good sale to match them up with, go ahead and use them before you lose them!

Savings sites such as Upromise (www.upromise.com) allow you to activate ecoupons for use at your local stores. At Upromise, though, the ecoupons will instead deposit money into a college savings account if you buy particular items using your store card. (See more on Upromise in Chapter 9.) In addition to these special ecoupons, Upromise offers a certain percentage of the sale price back on hundreds of other participating products, so plan to layer your Upromise ecoupons and savings with all of these other ways to save.

Last month, for example, I activated a handy ecoupon at Upromise: Save $1 for college when you buy Wacky Mac using your store loyalty card. After I loaded this ecoupon into my Upromise account, I saw a 75-cent coupon for Wacky Mac online, printed it out, and waited for a sale. A couple of weeks later, my local store put Wacky Mac on sale for $1 a bag. I walked in, used my 75-cent coupon to pay 25 cents for the bag, and earned $1 back into my Upromise account to save for college! You'll often see the Upromise logo in ads or even printed on paper manufacturer coupons, letting you know that this product participates in the program.

When stacking, also always look for ways to earn *overage*, the happy event when your savings total *more than the cost of the item.* Let's say that box of cereal we keep talking about is again on sale for $1.50. You have a higher-value manufacturer coupon you printed from the internet for $1 off a box. You also see 75 cents off that same brand and size of cereal when you go look at your Shortcuts ecoupons. When you use your paper coupon together with your ecoupon, you save $1.75 on a $1.50 box of cereal! In effect, you are *making* 25 cents on each box of cereal you buy.

Cereal	$1.50 per box (sale price)
Shortcuts coupon	- .75
Manufacturer coupon	-1.00
Your cost	- $.25

At most stores, this extra 25 cents will apply toward other items in your order (although some stores will adjust the coupon amount down to the actual cost of the item). Note that overage cannot apply toward sales tax, and the store won't give you money back. You need to have something else in your order to absorb that overage.

WHERE DO YOU FIND THESE COUPONS, ANYWAY?

There are so many places to find coupons! In the past, the Sunday newspaper inserts were your major (and sometimes only) source for coupons. These are still a great resource, but just be sure to subscribe to (or purchase) the paper in your city or region with the largest circulation. (The others won't have coupon inserts, or their inserts will include fewer coupons than the same inserts at their big-name competitor.) On a good coupon week, don't feel shy about buying multiple newspapers just for the coupon inserts. Let's say you spend $5 for five Sunday papers at $1 each, but you eventually use $10 in coupons out of each of those papers. This means that you'll save $50 over time on the items you buy with those coupons. That's a pretty good return on your initial investment!

Some stores, such as the Dollar Tree or Menards, sell Sunday papers for $1 (as opposed to, say, the $1.99 cover price for the *Chicago Tribune* when you buy it at grocery or drugstores). They also sell the early edition of the Sunday papers as soon as Saturday morning, allowing you to plan your trips and collect your coupons earlier. And if your family or neighbors don't use their Sunday coupons, why not ask them if you can have their inserts when they're done with their papers? Pay them back by giving them gifts from some of the great deals you find!

Did you know you can also find previews of upcoming coupon inserts online? This can be very handy as you plan your weekly shopping trips. If a fantastic coupon is coming out in Sunday's paper, you might want to wait a couple of days to purchase an item so that you can use that coupon on it. (Realize, though, that some coupons are regional, so these previews may not *exactly* match up with the coupons in your local paper. Don't buy multiple copies until you check the actual paper!) Here are a couple of places to check for coupon insert previews:

- Coupons, Deals and More (couponsdealsandmore.com)
- Taylortown Preview (www.taylortownpreview.com)

Visit these sites on Wednesday or Thursday to find that upcoming Sunday's coupon listings.

FIND COUPONS IN THE STORE

But don't stop with the Sunday inserts. When you start watching for them, you'll find coupons everywhere you look. Whenever I'm in a grocery store, I take a quick walk through the aisles looking for coupons and fill my pockets or purse as I go along. There are several different kinds of in-store

2010 and 2009 Coupon Insert Coupons

Remember, you may not receive the same coupons or the same denominations in your area. As a rule of thumb if you have doubles to 50¢ you will see a lot of 55¢ coupons. If you have doubles to 99¢, you will see a lot of $1 or $1/2 coupons. The best denominations for doubles come from Florida, SLC, Seattle, basically anyplace that does not have double coupons. The only exceptions seem to be the *Jersey Journal* (50¢ Saturday paper with full inserts with wonderful denominations) and the *AJC* As always, YMMV

I delete coupons as they expire!

Something that may confuse you about this listing... since I get coupons from all over the US I list a lot of denominations. You may see something like this:

Downy 25¢ or 50¢ or $1

That means for that week there were Downy coupons out in some areas at 25¢, some areas received 50¢ and some areas receive $1.

This helps people trade for the best possible coupon denomination in conjunction with the coupon policies in their area.

3/21/10

Smart Source

Aleve (40ct+) $1 *expires 6/30/10*
Aleve-D $1 *expires 6/30/10*
Alexia Frozen Item 55¢ or $1/2 *expires 5/2/10*
Alexia Select Sides 55¢ (**Thanks Hans**) or 75¢ or $1 *expires 5/2/10*
Alouette Brie Cheese $1 *expires 6/30/10*
Alouette Crumbled Cheese 50¢ *expires 6/30/10*
Alouette Soft Spreadable Cheese 75¢ *expires 6/30/10*
Arm & Hammer Oral Care Product $2.50/2 *expires 6/30/10*
Bayer Aspirin or Heart Health Advantage product (10ct+) $1 *expires 6/30/10*
Birds Eye Box or Bag Vegetables (excludes Steamfresh) 35¢ (**Thanks Hans**) or 50¢ or $1/3 *expires 4/17/10*
Birds Eye Steamfresh Premium Seafood Meals $1.50 *expires 5/1/10*
Birds Eye Steamfresh Vegetable, Pasta or Rice Variety 35¢ (**Thanks Hans**) or 50¢ or $1/3 *expires 4/17/10*
Bob Evans Sausage 25¢ or $1/2 *expires 5/23/10*
Bob Evans Side Dishes 35¢ or $1/2 *expires 5/23/10*
Breakstone's Sour Cream (16oz+) 55¢ or $1/2 *expires 4/25/10*
Buddig Deli Cuts (12 or 16oz) $1 *expires 6/30/10*
Cheerios Snack Mix 50¢ or $1/2 *expires 5/15/10*

Coupon insert listing from Coupons, Deals and More

coupons, with some extremely silly names. Knowing the lingo will be useful when you're reading online couponing sites and blogs that tell you the sorts of coupons to be on the lookout for. (Getting confused by all the lingo? Check out "Terms and Abbreviations to Know" at the end of the book.)

First, always look for *blinkies*. These are the coupons that pop out of the machines with little blinking lights that you find sticking out of store shelves. While you'll find these machines in stores, the coupons are actually put out by the manufacturers. The boxes aren't maintained by store personnel, so if they're empty, you'll just have to try back another day. Another silly yet memorable term, *peelies*, refers to coupons that are actually stuck to products. You can then peel these off to use on that particular product. These too are usually manufacturer coupons, but sometimes stores will stick on their own. You probably don't want to peel these off items that you're not buying on this particular shopping trip, though, because you run the risk of ripping the label and because the next person to come along will be disappointed when she buys an item with a missing sticker.

Look also for coupons hanging from the necks of products, or *hangtags*. These typically offer money off that product, but some hangtags include coupons for additional products manufactured by the same company. You'll also occasionally find a hangtag brochure with coupons for multiple products.

Product displays also often feature *tearpads* of coupons for the items on display—literally pads of coupons that you can tear from their backing. Tearpads might also contain multiple coupons for different items on a single sheet. These are especially popular around holidays. Around Memorial Day, for example, you're likely to find tearpads for charcoal, hot dogs, and pop. Also popular around particular times of year are recipe/coupon brochures, which you often find on endcap or stand-alone displays.

Collect hangtags, tearpads, brochures, and blinkies, even if you're not buying these items on your current shopping trip. Just bring them home and add them to your coupon file, then wait for the items to go on sale or for a matching electronic or store coupon to pop up. Use these strategically just as you use the coupons out of the Sunday inserts. You always want to match coupons with sales, no matter where those coupons come from. This is a fun game for older kids, too. Send them off on a (mannerly!) coupon hunt when you have them with you in the store. Another great way to get them involved!

Then there are *Catalinas*, which are those coupons that are printed out of a separate machine at the register after you make your purchase. As mentioned earlier, they are called Catalinas because that's the name of the company that makes the machines.

Catalina deals are my favorite deals at the grocery or drugstore. Why? Because I know these offer some great built-in money-back savings, even before I clip, print, or load a single coupon. One of my local stores, for instance, recently ran a "Buy $30 in participating items, get $15 back in Catalinas toward your next order" promotion. This is really like you're getting *50 percent savings right off the top.* Any coupons or additional savings you can stack on top of that? Gravy. Catalinas are always triggered on *pre-coupon* purchases, so even if you save $10 with coupons on that $30 required purchase, you'll still get your $15 back. The more you save in coupons, the better. If you save $10, you will pay just $20 and still get $15 back, bringing your net cost down to $5!

What's even better is that most stores let you "roll" the Catalinas from one transaction right into your next one. So I can take the $15 I just earned on one shopping trip, use it to help me buy another $30 of qualifying items, get my $15 back again, and repeat as often as I like.

How Do You Know When a Catalina Is Going to Print?

Catalinas, or similar coupons for money off your next order at the store, are one of the most important ways to *really* save. When good Catalina deals are running, you want to plan your purchases to take advantage of them. So how do you know when this is going to happen?

1. Catalinas are often advertised in the weekly store ads. Look in the midweek mailed ads (or in-store ads), as well as in the ads in the Sunday paper.

2. "Alerts" for Catalinas often print out at the store when you make another purchase.

3. In-store signs, shelf tags, or displays sometimes announce Catalina deals. Another reason to keep your eyes open in the store!

4. Deal blogs and forums cover Catalinas extensively. So pick someone to follow in your local area, and she should keep you in the know!

Unless products end up being free or close to free on these deals, don't buy things just because they're a good deal—buy items your family can actually use. Remember, there's always another deal!

Maximize your Catalina savings by staying as little over the required purchase amount as possible. If the deal says you need $30 of participating items to earn $15 back, you want to buy, say, $30 to $32 worth. Whether you spend $30 or $60 on these items, you'll still only get $15 back. Getting 50 percent back is great; getting 25 percent back is not as good. Don't spend too much on extra items you don't need. If you do want more, split your order into *two* $30 transactions so that you can get *two* $15 Catalinas! If a store says you need to buy "four or more" participating items to earn a Catalina, then buy just four—not five, not six, not 10. If you want more of these items, split them up into separate transactions so that you earn Catalinas on each trip.

 ## *Catalina Troubles?*

Catalinas can be notoriously tricky. Why?

- The machines that print these coupons are owned by the Catalina company, not by the store. So if they jam, lose their satellite transmission, or otherwise fail to print, stores often don't see that as their problem.

- Catalina deals are often not advertised or communicated to the frontline staff at the store. You might find out about them online, but if your coupon doesn't print, and you don't have an ad to point to, your customer service desk might not trust that you were really supposed to get the coupon back.

So what can you do if you know you were supposed to get a Catalina, but it didn't print?

- Try to resolve the issue while you're in the store. The cashier won't be able to help you, so take your receipt and your items to the customer service desk. Politely tell someone there that you thought you were supposed to get a Catalina coupon for this purchase and ask this person to please re-ring the items for you.

- If customer service can't or won't help you, and these are items you wouldn't have bought without the Catalina deal, you can return them then and there.

- You can also try contacting Catalina at 1-888-8COUPON, although it will take a day or two for your receipt to register in Catalina's system. Often the company will mail you the coupon you missed, but you'll end up putting in quite a bit of time on hold—and it's hit or miss whether you'll get a helpful customer service rep. Try this only if you're missing a high-value Catalina and don't want to let the matter drop.

PRINT MONEY FROM YOUR COMPUTER

I thought that "print money from your computer" would get your attention! But really, this is exactly what you're doing with printable coupons. Manufacturers like to offer printable coupons because you are using your own paper and your own ink, and they don't have to pay a newspaper to include their full-color coupons in the Sunday inserts. These coupons are also easy to track; manufacturers can offer a certain number of total prints online and be more confident that they'll reach their target audience (if you don't want it, you won't print it!) than when they pay to print a coupon in a newspaper that goes out to an entire geographic market. Online coupons also offer manufacturers a quick turnaround—they can get a coupon online within about a week, as opposed to the two or more months they need to get coupons into some print media. Online distribution of coupons was up 80 percent in 2008 alone and will only continue to rise.

These savings and flexibility also allow manufacturers to offer higher-value coupons online than they might place in the Sunday inserts. Sometimes the difference is just a few cents, but sometimes it represents significant savings. Recently, for example, I was able to print a coupon for $1 off Palmolive dish soap, while the coupon for Palmolive dish soap in the next week's Sunday paper was for just 25 cents off. That's a pretty significant difference, even when you factor in the cost of my paper and ink (which, of course, I buy on sale, taking advantage of coupons and rebates). I've also printed $1-off coupons for one box of cereal online, when the paper coupon that week was only for $1 off *three* boxes. Over time, the higher value of online coupons can add up to much bigger savings.

The two major coupon printing sites are:

- Coupons.com (www.coupons.com): This is the biggie. Consumers printed $313 million coupons from this site in the first 5 months of 2009 alone, beating the entire 2008 total.

- SmartSource.com (www.smartsource.com): SmartSource offers a different set of printable coupons than Coupons.com, so be sure to check both sites on a regular basis.

Each of these sites offers a number of identical coupons to every visitor and then additional regional coupons depending on the ZIP code you enter. Their coupons change at the beginning of the month, and then there are interim updates as a few new coupons are added and older ones reach their print limit or are removed. Always check around the first of the month to see what new coupons you can find. Deal bloggers also often point out the best new coupons available, helping you remember to go back and print.

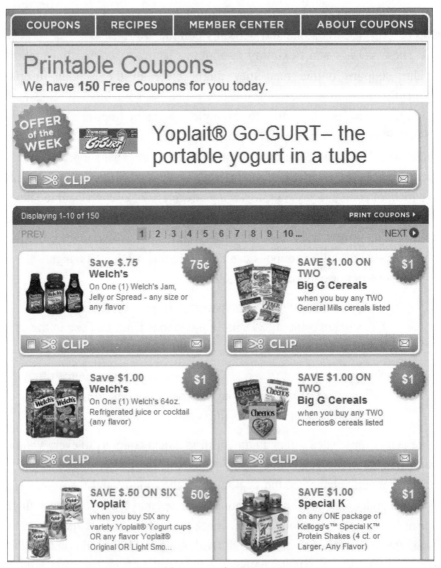

Printable coupons from Coupons.com

Printable Coupon Troubleshooting Tips

If you go to print a coupon from Coupons.com or another printable coupon website and find the coupon has disappeared, or if you have trouble printing it, there are several possible reasons.

1. *It has already hit its print limit.* When companies post coupons, they specify the number of total prints allowed. These print limits can sometimes be very small or will max out very quickly—sometimes in a matter of hours when it's a "hot" coupon (one for a popular product or one that makes an item very cheap or free). If you see a coupon you want, print it right away so that it doesn't hit its limit before you can get around to it.

2. *It is a regional deal.* Coupons.com, for example, asks you to put in a ZIP code. It will then show you a number of coupons available to everyone and some that are available only in certain regions of the country. So if you see a mention of a coupon that doesn't show up on your own list, it's possible it's only available in other areas. Could you put in a different ZIP code and see different coupons? Sure, but this is something you will need to decide the ethics on. Companies put out coupons targeted at specific ZIP codes to try to increase sales in a certain part of the country, just as they sometimes place regional coupons in newspapers in particular markets. While your store will be reimbursed for these coupons and the coupons themselves are legitimate, you circumvent their intent by using a different ZIP code.

3. *You have hit your individual print limit.* Sometimes you hit Print and the site will tell you "Sorry, you have already printed this coupon the number of times allowed," or it will start asking you to install the coupon printer over and over again. You may have printed this coupon a month ago, forgotten, and then tried again. Individual limits for coupons sometimes "reset" periodically, however, so you might try again in a week or two.

4. *You are trying to print from an Internet Explorer link in Firefox (or vice versa).* This happens a lot with BRICKS coupons from Coupons.com (you will see "bricks.coupons.com" in the address at the top of your screen). You will see "please wait," a blank screen, or repeated directions to install the coupon printer. To see if this is the problem, look at the horribly long web address up in the top bar of your browser. In the middle, you will see "bt=wg" or "bt=vi" or "bt=wi" or "bt=xs." Here, "wg" refers to Firefox, "vi" refers to Internet Explorer, "wi" refers to Internet Explorer, and "xs" refers to Safari (Mac). If you are using Internet Explorer and see "bt=wg" in your link, just change "wg" to "vi" or "wi" and try again to print. (Or use the appropriate two-letter combination for your own browser.)

BRICKS printable coupon link (Internet Explorer version)

5. *There's an issue between your computer and a given website.* A lot of people, for instance, have trouble with coupons

from SmartSource.com. (I can print them from my laptop, for example, but they completely crash my desktop computer.) Some report success by switching browsers—from Internet Explorer to Firefox or vice versa, for example. Note also that SmartSource coupons in particular tend to print very slowly and can take a minute or more to start printing, so don't close the window thinking that nothing is happening.

6. *It is a company error.* Sometimes things just go wrong, and coupons on a company's website randomly stop working— usually on a weekend, right when people want to print them to do a deal. If you have trouble on a given company's web- site, contact the company's customer support so that its web team can fix it, and sometimes it may mail you replacement coupons for your trouble.

Realize that some stores won't accept printable coupons due to concerns about coupon fraud, while some won't accept printable "free item" coupons or those over a certain dollar amount. You'll get to know your local stores' policies pretty quickly; many have them posted in the store or available on the website, or you can request them by contacting the store's corporate office.

Many sites will require that you install a small software application in order to print coupons. Don't worry; applications from legitimate sites like Coupons.com and SmartSource won't harm your computer. A major reason they require you to install this software is to limit the number of a specific coupon that can be printed from each computer (they usually let you print two, but sometimes the limit is one—or 10). This is another reason you can't print coupons from machines in public places such as libraries or FedEx/Kinkos—

even if they allowed you to install the software on their computers, you'd print your two coupons, then the next person who came along would be out of luck.

Another type of printable coupon is saved as a PDF file, which will load inside a free piece of software called Adobe Reader. Most computers now come with Reader installed, but if you need it on yours, you can download it at www.adobe.com/reader. The nice thing about PDFs is that you can print as many copies as you like (don't make photocopies, however; this is not allowed). Some stores, however, won't accept PDF printables because coupons printed from PDFs lack the extra protections of those printed with coupon software. To ensure that a PDF coupon is legit, check to make sure it's hosted on the company's own website. Look at the address in the address bar of your browser to see where it's coming from.

 ## Save on Ink and Paper

When you start printing a lot of coupons, you'll want to save as much as possible on ink and paper. Here are a few tips:

- If you have a color inkjet printer, set it to print in grayscale. Stores will take black-and-white coupons, and you don't want to waste your color ink, especially if you can refill your black and color cartridges separately.

- Buy ink on eBay (www.ebay.com). Yes, eBay! Cartridges and toner can be incredibly expensive at traditional office supply stores, but brand-new heavily discounted ink often shows up on eBay. Search for your printer model or the item number of your ink or toner cartridge to see what deals you can find.

- Try refilling your ink cartridges or purchasing refurbished toner. Check out sites such as Re-inks (www.re-inks.com). Stores like Walgreens also offer pretty regular cheap or free ink refill deals, so watch for announcements.

- Buy non-OEM ink. Nonbrandname ink generally works just as well and can be less than half the price.

- Stock up on copy paper in midsummer during a store's school supply deals.

- Buy paper when office supply stores offer "free after rebate" deals.

- Sign up for customer loyalty cards at office supply stores. These often give cash-back rewards each quarter for purchases made in store or online. Why not get the rebate on something you're buying anyway?

If you're not using printable coupons, you're throwing away the opportunity to save a whole lot of money at the store. I'd say that at least half the coupons I use each week are printed from the internet, simply because they're often higher in value and are more plentiful and varied than those that show up in the Sunday newspaper.

GET COUPONS FROM THE MANUFACTURER

Manufacturers often release printable coupons on their own websites. How do you find out about these? One way is by signing up for email newsletters or online communities straight from each manufacturer's website. Manufacturers let the people in their online community and on their newsletter list know first when new printable coupons are available. Some useful newsletters to sign up for include:

- Betty Crocker (www.bettycrocker.com/newsletters.htm): Sign up for several different newsletters; each contains different types of recipes, but all of them will take you to the same coupons each month.

- Kashi Connect (www.kashi.com/account/new): Get printable and mailed coupons and samples.

- Kraft Foods (www.kraftfoods.com): Click "sign up" in the upper right corner of the page to join the Kraft community.

- P&G Everyday Solutions (www.pgeverydaysolutions.com): Sign up to receive a newsletter and information on coupons, samples, and other promotions from P&G.

- Pillsbury (www.pillsbury.com/newsletters): Sign up for Pillsbury's regular newsletter or "cooking for 2" newsletter for smaller families. You will also receive monthly printable coupons.

- Stonyfield Farm (ecards.stonyfield.com/subscriptions.cfm): Get on this newsletter list to stay in the know about new organic coupons and Stonyfield Farm foods.

Check the websites of the manufacturers of your own favorite products to see what they might have available. These manufacturer coupons, especially higher-value ones, are also often linked from deal blogs and websites.

Another way to grab higher-value manufacturer coupons is by signing up for the manufacturers' "clubs." Manufacturers of baby products, in particular, often let you sign up on their sites to receive coupons for everything

Kashi online community

from diapers to infant formula in the mail. Some major baby product manufacturers to sign up with include:

- Gerber (www.gerber.com/public)

- Huggies (www.huggieshappybaby.com)

- Pampers (www.pampers.com/en_US/signup)

- Similac (similac.com/signup-similac)

Also be sure to check manufacturer sites for printable coupon offers. Sign up as well with store sites such as Babies R Us (https://secure.ed4.net/toysrus/preferencecenter/prefs.cfm) to receive info on promos and printable coupons.

ORDER COUPONS ONLINE

Ordering coupons online is something of a gray area. The fine print on most coupons says "not valid if transferred or sold," so order coupons online only at your own risk. Because of this risk, sellers are careful to stress that you are compensating them for their time in clipping and collecting, not for the coupons themselves. That being said, I have to mention this option here, because it's becoming more and more popular. Where can you get clipped coupons?

- Centsoff (www.centsoff.com): Sign up on this site for an email newsletter with news about new and hot coupons, shipping discount codes, and other useful info.

- The Coupon Clippers (thecouponclippers.com): This is the major coupon clipping site, and you can also sign up for its RSS feed of new coupons that have been added.

- Coupons & Things by Dede (www.couponsthingsbydede.com): Get both clipped coupons and entire inserts here.

- eBay (ebay.com): Search on eBay for the name of your product + the word *coupon*, and see what comes up.

If you need a certain coupon in bulk, these are good options.

If you're considering acquiring coupons online, think about your timing. Blogs and deal sites will let you know in advance when good deals are coming up at your local stores, giving you time to order and receive your coupons in plenty of time to use on a given sale. This is also an option if

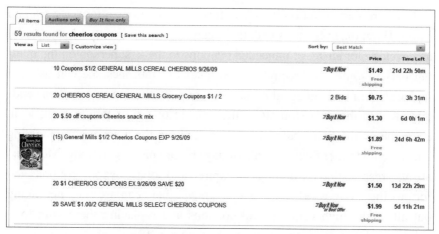

eBay search results for "Cheerios coupon"

your diet is limited by allergies or food sensitivities and you often need to purchase certain products in quantity because it lets you get multiple coupons for the same items.

If you just don't make it out to buy a paper, your Dollar Tree is sold out on a good coupon week, or you find yourself wishing later that you'd bought more in a good week, you can also buy entire coupon inserts online. Coupons & Things by Dede provides both whole coupon inserts and clipped coupons.

You can also trade coupons with others online. Maybe you have a baby but not a dog, so why not trade the dog food coupons from your local paper with someone who has no need for their diaper coupons? Most of the bargain forums offer trading boards and a system of rating member traders. Rating systems at these sites and on eBay help you know whether you're dealing with a reputable seller or trader and whether the coupons you receive will be legitimate.

If you're part of an online deals forum, you can also look for *coupon trains*. Here, the train starts with the organizer, or *conductor*, who mails out an envelope, or *envie*, of unneeded coupons to the first person on the mailing list, or *route*. The recipient then takes out the ones she can use and replaces them with an equal number of coupons she can't use—then sends the envie to the next stop along the line. In order for this to work well, everyone on the train route has to agree to keep the train moving, holding the envie no longer than a couple of days before passing it along. Members are also responsible for pulling out expired and soon-to-expire coupons and for passing along good coupons they know others can use (i.e., not taking out all of the high-value, useful coupons and replacing them with low-value, "junk" coupons that few people can use). Trains can get more complicated if members share "wish lists" of specific coupons they need, and members often keep in touch about related topics through messaging each other on their forum or through email.

DOWNLOAD MOBILE COUPONS

A newer approach to coupons allows you to load them right onto your cell phone, then hand it to the cashier to scan your screen at checkout. This way, no one wastes paper and ink! A major player here is Cellfire, which allows users both to load coupons onto their mobile phones and to load them onto their store loyalty cards.

Some stores are starting to give out mobile coupons as incentives to load their applications onto your smartphone. As I type, for instance, Barnes & Noble is offering a mobile coupon for a free tall Starbucks coffee at its in-store café when you download its free iPhone application—just show the cashier the coupon on your screen. I got mine last week, and it was even tastier because it was free! Barnes & Noble probably won't be offering the same deal by the time you read this, but look for similar offers to be popping up all over as the popularity of smartphones, apps, and coupons continues to grow. Starbucks itself runs similar offers: Users can either print out a coupon or display it to their barista on-screen. Save paper, ink, trees, and time! Target recently introduced mobile coupons that subscribers can receive via text message.

Coupon Karma

What comes around, goes around, in couponing as in life. Sometimes your cashier will be having a bad day and will take it out on you. Sometimes, she'll be concerned that you're somehow cheating the store by using coupons improperly. Some stores also "grade" their cashiers by how fast they move customers through their lines—and you and your pile of coupons are sure to slow the process down. Be considerate and take what steps you can to make everything go as smoothly as possible. If you have a coupon for a free item, for example, the cashier will have to write in the price. So make a note of this price yourself or give her the coupon when she scans the item so she can note the price right then instead of having to roll back the register tape or screen at the end. Make sure you use only coupons that match up to items in your order, and don't crease, tear, spill things on, or otherwise mess up the bar code that allows a coupon to be scanned easily.

To help avoid concerns about coupon fraud, always do your best to avoid using coupons in an unethical manner. More stores are becoming leery of printable coupons—and with good reason, since printables are easier for unethical consumers to alter or misuse. Be careful yourself to avoid online printable offers that look too good to be true. If an online coupon looks as if it has been altered or otherwise seems suspicious, stay away. Recent frauds have caused stores to tighten up their coupon policies and to scrutinize printables ever more closely. If you are suspicious about whether an online coupon is legitimate, you can check with the Coupon Information Corporation (www.cents-off.com).

Realize also that you can *never, ever* photocopy a printable coupon in order to use it multiple times or give it to friends. This is coupon fraud and

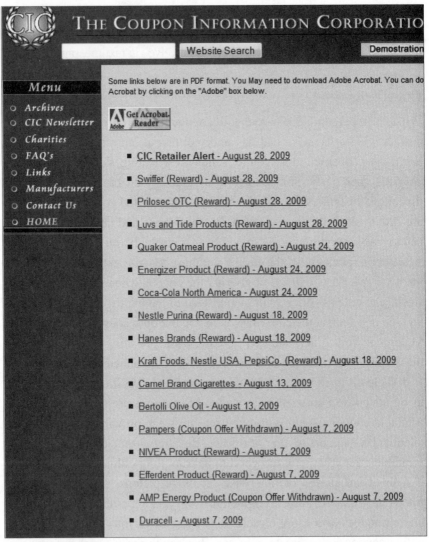

Fraudulent coupon list from the Coupon Information Corporation

is illegal. When you install the software that allows you to print coupons from your computer, one of the things it does is record your computer's information right onto the printed coupon. In this way, companies can track it back to you if there's a widespread problem with a copied or altered coupon—so just don't do it!

Another unethical act is to deliberately use a coupon for a product it's not intended for. Some coupons, for instance, are coded so that they work on any item from a manufacturer, even if the wording on the coupon makes it very clear that it's only intended for use on a *particular* item. Some unscrupulous sites make a habit of telling users how to fraudulently use these higher-value coupons to get lower-value items for free (no, I'm not going to tell you who they are). Just don't do it. The unethical use of coupons hurts all of us because in response, stores tighten up on their coupon policies and manufacturers think twice about the coupons they release.

When you see coupons in the store, be sure to leave some for others. Don't take an entire tearpad of coupons, for instance, either for your own use or to list on eBay. (And if you see an eBay seller listing hundreds of identical coupons you saw on a tearpad in your own store, that may tell you something about your seller's ethics!) On the other side of things, you can think about being a "coupon fairy." Coupon fairies leave coupons in the aisle for others to discover. If you have a stack of coupons for diapers, but your kids are teenagers, think about leaving a few in the baby aisle the next time you shop. If you find coupons for free dog or cat food but don't have pets, either leave these near the items in the store or buy the products to donate to your local animal shelter.

GIVE IT AWAY

Now let's step back. Besides being ethical in how we use our coupons, we can use our savings to help others in tough economic times. Sometimes, as with that free pet food, you'll see sales on items that just seem too good to pass up. You might be able to buy something for free or nearly free, but you know your family won't use it. Maybe you don't actually need another five tubes of free toothpaste when there are already 10 under the sink. Maybe your kids gag at the very thought of eating brand X cereal, but it's free this week after coupon. Get it anyway!

Food pantries, women's shelters, homeless shelters, crisis pregnancy centers, animal shelters, and other service organizations are in serious need of donations in tough economic times: Usage is up, while donations are down, and these organizations aren't going to care if donated items were purchased for pennies on the dollar. As Alli D., a couponer and mother of two, says, "The most important tips I would give are to save your coupons, stockpile when you can get things cheap or free, buy the free stuff at CVS and/or Walgreens even though you may not need it today, and donate the extra. Sometimes you can only get things for free by buying seven. There are lots of hungry people out there who can benefit from your free purchases." You truly "win" at the grocery and drugstore game when you use your savings to help others. Jenny S., suburban mom of two, says of her couponing efforts that "for the first time ever, I got to donate food to the local food pantry. That was the most amazing feeling. I try to do it as often as I can."

Other couponers have been able to help out struggling friends and family who are more likely to accept goods than actual money. Helen T, who enjoys saving money in her free time, shares: "We keep the items we know we can use before they expire. We then donate to homeless shelters, food pantries, church friends that need a hand, coworkers who deal with prison ministries or have large families. By purchasing these items (or being paid to get them!) we can help more than if we just wrote a check. It feels good to be able to hand a friend at church a bag of groceries as they are more likely to accept this than cash." And Jen F., a part-time librarian and mom to two boys, explains that "it's been really rewarding for me, personally, in that I am able to give above and beyond what I would normally give as a result of couponing. My family and I have been buying groceries for a needy family that I know through work, and I am able to surprise them with bags of groceries and goodies for very little money. The joy is inexplicable."

How can you find places to donate? Sometimes I don't even make it out of the grocery store; I just throw items into the local food pantry bin on the way out. See if your store has one of these by the door (some may do this only around the Thanksgiving and Christmas holidays). Local public libraries occasionally run a regular "food for fines" campaign, in which fines are forgiven in return for each nonperishable donation you bring in. Find out whether your library does this, and if not, it might be a great win-win program to suggest. The U.S. postal service also holds an annual food drive, in which you can leave nonexpired, nonperishable items alongside your mailbox. You can look up food banks across the country at Feeding America (feedingamerica.org/foodbank-results.aspx). Click through to the one that serves your local area; that site will likely list places to donate.

Does your church run a food pantry or mission program? This is another great outlet for these sorts of items. Also see whether your church or other organization sponsors regular programs such as a mitten tree at Christmas or backpacks of school supplies each fall. You can put aside items for these types of programs all year when you're able to buy them at their cheapest, which lets you donate as much as possible.

Charitable donations of goods to nonprofit organizations are also tax deductible; just be sure to get a receipt to document your donation if you want to claim it for tax purposes and to keep your own store receipts as documentation. If you decide to use your savings on groceries and toiletries as more disposable income to let you make cash donations, you can research your charities at Charity Navigator (charitynavigator.org) to find out how responsibly they use their funds. If you decide to donate some of the time you're saving toward a good cause, check sites like VolunteerMatch (www.volunteermatch.org) to find local volunteer opportunities.

Another way to give online is through sites that offer donations for your clicks. Kraft Foods, for example, ran a "Share a Little Comfort" campaign in the summer of 2009 that donated 10 boxes of macaroni and cheese every time someone clicked on its site. These sorts of campaigns are a win-win situation for the companies who run them: They draw your attention to their sites and their brands while also giving to a worthy cause. Other sites do similar click-through programs, in which clicks are sponsored and each click earns donations for an organization or cause. The Animal Rescue Site (www.theanimalrescuesite.com), for instance, has a click-to-give pro-gram—you click on the site daily, and sponsors provide food and care to rescued animals. Check the other tabs at the top of the site for other click-to-give opportunities, including everything from mammograms to habitat protection.

The Animal Rescue Site

You can also donate your expired coupons! Military families stationed overseas are able to use coupons on base up to 6 months past their expiration date, so if none of your local stores accept expired coupons, pass them on to people who can use them—and who are serving our country. You can find a list of bases that accept these coupons at GrocerySavingTips.com (www.grocerysavingtips.com/expiredgrocerycoupons.htm), or you can sign up to "adopt" a base to send your coupons to at the Overseas Coupon Program site (www.ocpnet.org).

Take the opportunity to pass your savings on to others. When you learn to save, you also enable yourself to give. Use the items you have stockpiled on the cheap to help friends and family who have fallen on hard economic times, whether you just cook them a few meals or share part of your abundance with others. Barbara G., a private music teacher, says, "Many times, I have been able to go shopping from my stockpile for friends and family that need a little to get by with. It has blessed us to be able to give in that way and be prepared to do so when needs arise."

5

Get It Online

Now that you're saving on almost everything you buy at the store, you can start saving on everything online. What do I find, buy, and do online? Everything! I find everything from discounts on restaurant gift certificates to free TV shows online; it truly is the *World Wide* Web. So why not branch out and explore your options? Move beyond your local stores to maximize your savings on everything with the strategic use of online resources. Use online alternatives to pricey software, entertainment, and educational options—and find alternatives to everything from traditional phone service to traditional TV service.

Buying online can often be your best bet if you live in a more remote area that doesn't have multiple competing stores. Check out Amazon.com's grocery section (www.amazon.com; choose "grocery" from the menu), Drugstore.com, and a number of other online retailers. Their deals can often beat the prices at local stores, especially in rural areas, where there's a lack of local competition to bring prices down and give you more shopping options. The internet *is* their competition. Online deals for organic products, gluten-free products, and other specialty items can also sometimes beat local stores' offerings, so if you're shopping for special dietary needs, be sure to explore online options for the products and brand names you need.

But why stop at just buying *things* online? Do you want to watch your favorite TV shows? Play games? Find educational activities for your kids? It's all there. You can move your phone service online to save hundreds of dollars per year—which you can then use to help pay for that all-important high-speed internet access. You can find everything from restaurant discounts to reviews of local companies to customized radio stations online—all of which help you save money, time, and hassle. You'll wonder why you never thought of doing most of this before!

BUY IT ONLINE

Let's start with buying things online. We've all heard of the heavyweights in the online shopping arena, such as Amazon.com and eBay. But what about your smaller, specialty retailers? Move beyond the big guys to get discounts on just about anything you can think of, as well as access to a lot of items you can't find locally.

What have I bought online? Everything from my son's desk to shoes to books to back-to-school backpacks. And oh, those shoes. OK, I do like shoes. I don't even wear all the ones I have, but I admire them so. If you, too, admire shoes, get yourself over to Shoebuy.com (www.shoe buy.com) and sign up for its email list to get regular percent-off discounts. Why am I such a fan of Shoebuy.com? Because, besides the selection and prices, it has *free shipping both ways.* This means that if you order a pair of shoes and the shoes don't fit, you can send them right back at no cost to you. Because shipping is often the deal killer online and because shoes are one of those things you have to try on to make sure you can use them, this is fantastic—and I've taken advantage of it more than once!

Shoebuy.com

You'll often find better deals on smaller or niche sites, where companies make money selling a small number of products in volume. You can also find some interesting products that aren't available at your local stores. Get a unique gift or try something new.

As far as the big guys go, start by thinking about the stores where you shop in person. Check out their websites to see what else they offer. Most of these stores have email newsletters in which they send out regular discounts and sale information, so be sure to sign up. Here are just a few of the lists that I'm on myself:

- The Children's Place (www.childrensplace.com): Use the signup on the webpage, and you'll get regular emails with discount codes, clearance sale info, and printable coupons to use in-store.

- JC Penney (www3.jcpenney.com/jcp/emailupdates.aspx): Get emails with info about sales, coupon and free-shipping codes, and printable coupons.

- Kohl's (www.kohls.com/upgrade/registration/sale_alert_ signup.jsp): You'll get a printable $5-off coupon to use in-store just for signing up, plus regular emails with discount codes, printable coupons, and sale info.

Visit the websites of all your favorite stores and look for ways to sign up to stay in the know. As always, you might want to use a free email account for anything you sign up for online.

You can also use sites like Overstock (www.overstock.com) and GraveyardMall.com (www.graveyardmall.com) to find liquidation deals on various items. Watch the shipping at GraveyardMall.com, though, because sometimes it can be more than the cost of the item. Overstock is more reasonable and often offers free shipping to new customers and other shipping discounts.

Lastly, be sure not to miss Woot (www.woot.com). This one-day-one-deal site lists a new discounted item each day with flat $5 shipping. Last year, we bought a refurbished Dyson vacuum at half the price of new. (And yes, it really does suck up a disgusting amount of filth from carpets you thought were clean, just like in the commercials!) Woot's sister site, Kids.Woot (kids.woot.com), does the same one-day-one-deal offers for kids' items.

Pay It With PayPal

When you buy or sell online, you'll eventually need to get yourself a PayPal account (www.paypal.com). PayPal, which is owned by eBay, allows users to buy and sell items online without exposing their personal credit card data or signing up for a pricey merchant account. Some smaller shops *only* take PayPal, and it's the commonly accepted form of currency on eBay.

Consumers can sign up for a PayPal account and then use their PayPal funds to safely purchase items online. Sellers can sign up, have payments deposited directly into their PayPal account, and then withdraw those funds by check or direct deposit into their bank account.

While there are a couple of competitors to PayPal, not enough people really use them yet to make it worth your time in most cases. So get a PayPal account and get shopping!

SUPPORT OTHER WORK-AT-HOME FOLKS

Looking for creative and unique gifts? Try Etsy (www.etsy.com). While Etsy is also a great way for crafters to *make* money (and something to think about yourself, if you're crafty), one big way that we can support one another in our money-saving, money-making endeavors is by supporting independent businesses large and small. The crafters on Etsy, "your place to buy and sell all things handmade," work for themselves and are able to use the combined power of Etsy to reach a wide audience for their products. Etsy's search function is really handy here. Let's say that you have a

Kids.Woot

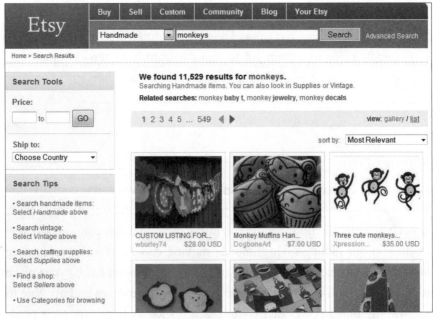

Etsy search for "monkeys"

friend who collects monkey-themed items. Just type in *monkeys*, and you'll find everything monkey-related: magnets, T-shirts, stuffed animals, earrings, hand-painted plates, tote bags, decorations, stationery, and more.

eBay (ebay.com) is another option for finding independent sellers to support. Not only do many independent sellers list auction items on eBay, but you'll notice that when you search for items, you'll often see links to eBay stores. These stores are set up by individuals or companies to sell a variety of products, and a number of them are run by other work-at-home folks.

eBay offers both auction items you can bid on and "buy it now" items with a set price. When you're bidding in eBay auctions, you might look at using free auction "sniping" tools such as BidNip (www.bidnip.com), AuctionStealer (www.auctionstealer.com), and Auction Sniper (www.auctionsniper.com). These tools automatically put in bids for you at the last second so that you don't have to sit in front of the computer waiting for an auction to end and hope that you're fast enough to outbid the competition. Some offer a certain number of free "snipes" per month, so if you're a low volume bidder, you should be fine.

RESEARCH BEFORE YOU BUY

Online product reviews are fantastic for getting a real person's opinion of a product before buying it (rather than just a marketer's spin). While Amazon.com is the leader here—find reviews on Amazon.com for just about any book you can think of, as well as many other products—a number of other sites offer or collect reviews for your use. Use sites such as Buzzillions (www.buzzillions.com) and Epinions (www.epinions.com) to see what other people have to say about whether a product holds up well, whether it's hard to put together, or whether it tastes good, looks good, or fits true to size; use their opinions to help you decide which products to buy. Remember, though, that people are always more likely to take the time to post a review when they're mad about something!

You can also use these reviews to help you sort through local services online. Finding reliable service is hard, but the power of online community makes it slightly easier. Just as people review products online, they also share their experiences with local companies, restaurants, and service providers, getting them out there for the whole world to see. Use sites like:

- Citysearch (www.citysearch.com)

- Yahoo! Local (local.yahoo.com)

- Yelp (www.yelp.com)

Each of these carries reviews from your neighbors about local services and restaurants.

You can also check out specialized review sites for any type of service you need. Look at TripAdvisor (www.tripadvisor.com) for reviews of hotels, restaurants, and more, and use sites such as Urbanspoon (www.urbanspoon.com) to see restaurant reviews from both critics and regular diners. (Urbanspoon also has a handy iPhone app to help you find restaurants when you're out and about or out of town.)

GET DISCOUNTS ON EVERYTHING

When you want to buy something online or find out whether you can get something cheaper online than in-store, never grab the first offer you see and always check for coupon codes and discounts before purchasing. Several sites offer price comparisons and consumer reviews, while others provide discount and free shipping codes for various online merchants. Use the comparison shopping sites to make sure you're getting the best deal on things you buy online. These sites compare prices across a number of online retailers, but be sure you consider shipping costs, too, because these can vary widely from store to store. Most comparison sites also provide

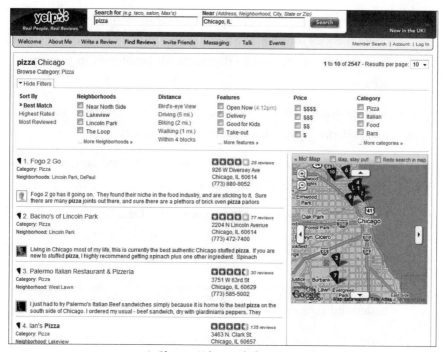

A Chicago Yelp search for "pizza"

user ratings of these retailers to help you make sure you're buying from a reliable outlet.

Once you have picked a store to buy from, you can use coupon code sites to search for discount codes for that retailer. Use these on your order to get free shipping or a percentage off. These codes can save you a bundle and take only a few minutes to find. I recently saved 25 percent plus $9.95 in shipping costs on a new school backpack and lunch tote for my son from Land's End, just by spending a little quality time searching for discount codes online.

Useful coupon code and comparison shopping sites include:

- CouponCabin (www.couponcabin.com): In addition to looking up coupon codes for online retailers, you can enter your ZIP code to find printable coupons and discounts for businesses in your local area.

- CouponWinner.com (www.couponwinner.com): Search for codes and coupons by retailer, or browse by category.

- Currentcodes.com (www.currentcodes.com): Find current coupon codes for more than 2,000 online stores.

- DealTime.com (www.dealtime.com): Use DealTime's comparison shopping search engine to compare prices across multiple stores and read product reviews from other users.

- FreeShipping.org (www.freeshipping.org): Find free shipping codes and sign up for email alerts of new codes.

- Froogle (www.froogle.com): Search for products across multiple sites so that you can find the retailer with the lowest price.

- mySimon (www.mysimon.com): Search or browse by category and check out "daily shopping picks" of hot deals.

- NexTag (www.nextag.com): Use the best feature of this comparison search site, TruePrice, which lets you enter your ZIP code to instantly calculate tax and shipping for easier comparison among stores.

- PriceGrabber.com (www.pricegrabber.com): Enter your email address to be alerted when a product's price drops.

- RetailMeNot.com (www.retailmenot.com): Search the collection of discount and free shipping codes from users, who are also invited to weigh in on whether these codes worked for them. It now also has a printable coupon search!

- Spoofee.com (www.spoofee.com): Search for codes or find Spoofee's "hottest" deals and codes right on the front page. Also click on the Free Goods tab to find freebies listed by their forum members.

Why have I listed so many of these? Because they all have their strengths and weaknesses, and because some list codes that others miss, some include higher-value codes for certain stores, and one might find a sale before another has updated its listings. So always make sure you search on more than one site for both discount codes and comparison shopping. Pick three or four favorites and check them regularly whenever you're buying something online. If all else fails, you can try Google for coupon codes—type in the name of your store and "coupon code" or "discount code."

Another site I like is Price Protectr (www.priceprotectr.com). Like regular retail stores, online stores often have a price guarantee for a certain

RetailMeNot.com

time after purchase. Find the item cheaper a week later? Get refunded the difference. Price Protectr helps you track these price changes. Just enter the link to the product information and your email address, and it will email you if a lower price turns up. This can also be really helpful if you're not sure about whether to buy an item or if it's priced a bit too high for your blood. Just put the info into Price Protectr, and wait for the price to drop.

GET PAID BACK FOR BUYING ONLINE

If you're doing any shopping online, you'll also want to sign up for one or more online rebate sites. After you have created an account on one of these sites, when you shop through it, the site gives you back a percentage of the purchases you make after clicking through from the rebate site to a participating merchant. For instance, if you start at a rebate site, click on its Old Navy link, then buy something on the Old Navy website, and a percentage of what you spend will be deposited right into your account on the online rebate site.

Getting paid to buy stuff online seems backwards, doesn't it? But the trick here is to only take advantage of such programs *if you are using them to purchase items you're going to be buying anyway.* Never buy something just because it has a nice rebate on it, because you still have to spend money on the deal. However, if you are already planning to purchase an item online (especially a big-ticket purchase), doing so through an online rebate link only makes sense. Why *not* get some money back on something you already plan on buying?

Some of the major rebate sites include:

- Bing cashback (www.bing.com/cashback)
- Cashbaq (www.cashbaq.com)
- Ebates (www.ebates.com)

- Extrabux (www.extrabux.com)

- FatWallet (www.fatwallet.com)

- Mr. Rebates (www.mrrebates.com)

- Shop at Home (www.shopathome.com)

Each site works basically the same way: Every time you click through from one of these sites to a participating etailer (online retailer), you earn back a percentage of your purchase into your account. When you hit a certain amount, you can cash out via check or PayPal. These sites often offer a bonus for signing up (typically about $5), and some offer referral programs in which, when friends sign up under you, you get a percentage of each of their rebates! You can browse through these sites' lists of participating stores, search for a specific store, or search for a specific item to see which participating store carries it.

You might want to sign up for more than one rewards program, because some include different stores than others, and some offer higher rebates on some stores than others. (Also, why not get the signup bonus at more than one place?) After you've found out which one best fits your needs and includes the stores you shop at most, though, it is a good idea to pick one to use consistently for your online purchases across the year. Around the holidays, cash your rebates in for an instant Christmas fund to buy gifts for your family.

Rebate portals also often offer coupon codes right on their sites to give you extra savings, so be sure to check the sites to see whether a code is available for the retailer you want to use. Be aware, though, that using a coupon code from another site might cause conflicts: You may not get the rebate as expected.

Some credit card companies have similar rebate sites for purchases made through their credit card. Check to see what might be available for your card (but don't sign up for a credit card just to get cash back through online rebates). When you're buying something online through a third-party rebate site, you can always use a rewards credit card to get your credit card rewards *plus* the reward from the rebate site. Stack your money-back offers, just like you stack different types of savings at the grocery store! The college savings site Upromise (www.upromise.com) offers a similar rebate program, but rebates here are put into your account for college savings. You can then add those funds to your own or your child's 529 account. (I'll tell you more about Upromise in Chapter 9, because it's just a fantastic program that I use myself.)

Get Paid Back for Buying in General

While we're talking about rebates, let me mention mail-in rebates, too. Some people don't bother with these types of rebates, figuring that the time and effort involved aren't worth the payback. I always send away for them (unless it's not worth the cost of my time and the stamp, which is basically anything under $2)—partially because I *know* companies use rebate offers with the full knowledge that many purchasers will never take advantage of that rebate. (And you already know that I don't like companies to get away with stuff!)

Rebates also let you try products that you might not normally buy. Use a "try me free" rebate to try out a new cleaning product, a new type of food, or a new baby product. While it may take 6 to 8 weeks, you'll get your money back eventually. In addition, rebates almost always give you back the purchase price *before any coupons you use*, so when you use a coupon on a product for which you also have a rebate offer, you can actually make money (or at least pay for that stamp).

So where do you find rebate opportunities? Many deal blogs do regular roundups of them (mine are posted on Tuesdays). The blog Coupons, Deals and More maintains a huge listing of printable rebate forms (couponsdeals andmore.com/printable-refunds-rebates) that you can browse through to see if any of the offers entice you to try one of these products.

One nice option is the introduction of new online "easy rebates." Staples does this (www.stapleseasyrebates.com). Just enter the codes from your receipt into its online rebates site, and Staples will process the rebate for you—no messing with stamps or filling out forms by hand. Watch for more stores to offer online rebates to save both you and them some hassle.

THINK OUTSIDE THE BOX

What else can you buy online? How about gift cards at a discount! Sites like GiftCardsAgain.com (giftcardsagain.com) sell gift cards to popular stores at a discount. Check there if you're planning on making a major purchase at a local retail store. You can buy a discounted (generally 5 percent to 20 percent) gift card on the site, then use the card at your local store to pay for your items. You've just given yourself a present of an extra percent-off discount!

You can do it the other way around, too, which is especially useful around the holidays. If you receive a gift card for a store you don't like (and you don't want to re-gift it), you can sell it to the companion site GiftCardBuyBack.com (giftcardbuyback.com) for 60 percent to 80 percent of its face value.

GET PHONE SERVICE ONLINE

Tired of paying those high monthly phone bills? Why not ditch your landline entirely? (This can also help you put money aside to pay for that all-important internet access.) Some people rely solely on their cell phones, now that most cell plans come with huge numbers of minutes and free long distance service, but this option is best if you live in an apartment or smaller house and don't have younger kids without their own phones.

Your other option is to switch to a Voice Over Internet Protocol (VoIP) service (basically, phone calls over the internet), which lets you make phone calls without paying those pesky monthly fees to the phone company. VoIP quality and reliability have grown, and VoIP offers huge savings over traditional phone service, but it requires a high-speed internet connection. Your three main options are Vonage (www.vonage.com), magicJack (www.magicjack.com), and Skype (www.skype.com). Here's the basics of how they differ (prices noted are current as of February 2010).

Vonage offers a variety of residential plans, but its Vonage World plan gives you unlimited local and long distance U.S. phone calls, plus free calls to 60 countries for $24.99 per month (plus taxes and fees, with a 1-year contract). You can keep your current phone number, you can use your existing phone (with the adapter they send you), and the plan includes several features as standard that the phone company dings you for each month: call waiting, caller ID, anonymous call block, voice mail, three-way calling, and more. Vonage also offers a more basic plan that includes 500 minutes of local and long-distance calling to Canada, the U.S., and Puerto Rico— as well as the standard features—for $17.99 a month.

The magicJack service gives you unlimited local and long distance calling to the U.S., Puerto Rico, the U.S. Virgin Islands, and Canada for $19.95 per year and includes features such as caller ID, call waiting, call forwarding, and more as standard. Simply plug magicJack into your computer and plug your phone into the other end. The catch? You can't keep your phone number. You can sign up at the magicJack site for a free 30-day trial to see whether it meets your needs. You pay an up-front $39.95 charge for the magicJack device, get the first year of calls for free, and then pay $19.95 per year thereafter. You can purchase international calling minutes online through your personal magicJack account.

Skype lets you make *free* Skype-to-Skype video phone calls and conference phone calls to others over the internet using your computer—but the other callers also have to install Skype. Even so, Skype is great, especially the video feature, if you're calling distant relatives. Set grandma up with Skype, sit the kids down in front of your webcam, and call her so they can see each other from afar! If you want to use Skype as more of a traditional phone service, you can either pay as you go or sign up for a variety of subscription plans, for example, unlimited outbound calls to landlines and cell phones in the U.S. and Canada for $2.95 per month. If you want to get an online number so that people can call you, you incur another charge, but it is 50 percent off if you have a monthly subscription. Also, you can't keep your current phone number.

If you're not ready to get rid of your landline, you can still look for cheaper alternatives to your current service. Use sites like PhoneRate Finder.com (www.phoneratefinder.com) to help you find the best plan. When it comes to cell phones, MyRatePlan (myrateplan.com) and BillShrink (www.billshrink.com) will help you compare cell phone plans to find the best one for your needs. Why pay monthly for extra services you're not using? And if you hardly use your cell phone, think about switching to a prepaid service. Why pay a monthly fee for minutes you never use?

And I hope you're never calling 411 to get info! It now charges more than $1 for each lookup. Try using online services like Switchboard (www.switchboard.com) or call 1-800-FREE-411. This advertising-supported service gives you free 411 info—after you listen to a brief ad. You can listen to that ad while cooking dinner or changing a diaper or otherwise multitasking—who's to know? Or try Google's free service, 1-800-GOOG-411 (and watch the video demo at www.google.com/ goog411).

BUY ONLINE, EAT LOCALLY

I love, love, love eating out. Food just always tastes better when someone else makes it. This is another area in which your family may complain of feeling "deprived," especially if they've grown used to a steady diet of takeout while you've been working full-time. So how do you get the best deal on your (occasional) restaurant outing?

First, you really must check out Restaurant.com (www.restaurant.com). This site offers *major* discounts on gift certificates to local restaurants (although these discounts often come with certain restrictions, such as being good only at lunch, only for dine-in orders, only on certain nights of the week, or only good on a specific minimum purchase—so read the fine print). Furthermore, Restaurant.com regularly puts out promo codes that get you even better discounts. I've seen the discounts go as low as a $25 gift certificate for $2! (And I always post these on MashupMom.com.)

Sites such as DinnerBroker (www.dinnerbroker.com) work a bit differently. They offer 10- to 30-percent discounts when you make a reservation to dine during off-peak periods, which is great for anyone who needs to get home early to the babysitter. You also earn points by making reservations through the site or referring friends, which can then be used to buy gift certificates for participating restaurants. (Whether you use DinnerBroker or not, you can often save just by shifting your dining out patterns. The same items often cost much less when they're listed on a lunch rather than on a dinner menu, for example, so why not make your midday meal your big one?)

Also, never throw away those newspaper inserts, midweek ads, or little coupon envelopes that come in the mail without looking at them. Restaurants are feeling the economic pinch as heavily as anyone else, so they are issuing paper coupons to help entice people back in to eat. Some of these coupons are also now available online. Valpak, which mails out local coupons, has a companion website (www.valpak.com) where you can print local coupons for everything from restaurants to carpet cleaning.

Be sure to sign up online for loyalty or birthday clubs at as many local restaurants as possible. Perks here include such things as free meals, discounts, or appetizers in your birthday month; printable buy-one-get-one-free coupons; and loyalty points you can turn in for free appetizers or other prizes. Check out the Free Food Events group on Facebook (www.face book.com/group.php?gid=11708023385) for more on birthday clubs, coupons, and special events. (More on restaurant freebies later.)

You might also invest in your local Entertainment Book (www. entertainment.com). These books come out annually and contain coupons for restaurants, stores, attractions, and more, all in your local area. And when you buy the print copy, you also get special access to additional print-able coupons and discounts online. You'll easily get your money's worth and more. Other ideas? Go back to GiftCardsAgain.com, because it also sells discounted restaurant gift cards to popular chains. And check out KidsMealDeals.com (kidsmealdeals.com) for "kids eat free" days at restaurants in your area.

DOWNLOAD OR USE IT ONLINE

I use many *free* online or downloadable alternatives to pricey software. Most people never use all the bells and whistles in the expensive software they pay for, so these stripped-down, free alternatives work out fine. And sometimes, free software or web applications can do just about anything their expensive cousins can do! Here are just a few that I use:

- To edit photos for family or for my blog, I use Picnik (www.picnik. com). This online editor lets you crop, brighten, resize, and other-wise edit photos to your heart's content, right in your web browser.

- To share photos with family and friends without having to email big files back and forth, I use Flickr (www.flickr.com), which lets me organize, share, and tag my photos with keywords for easy retrieval later.

- Then there's security software. For antivirus protection, I use AVG (free.avg.com). For spyware protection, I use Spybot (www.safer-networking.org). For adware protection, I use Ad-Aware (www.lavasoft.com). For a firewall, I use ZoneAlarm (www.zonealarm.com). All of these keep my computer humming along and protect me from security threats online.

- To write a document together with someone far away, I use Google Docs (docs.google.com) and do it all online. I've also used the OpenOffice suite (www.openoffice.org), which is a free, downloadable full-featured alternative to Microsoft Office. Both Google Docs and OpenOffice let you save documents in Microsoft Word format so that you can share them with others who use that program.

Find thousands of other programs—and reviews—at CNET's Download.com (www.download.com).

READ IT ONLINE

Are you still subscribing to your local newspaper? Publishers are probably glad that *someone* is, but you can get your news and information online just as easily. (Be sure to buy that Sunday paper, though, because you need your coupon inserts!) You can use sites such as BugMeNot (www.bugme not.com) to bypass registration requirements if you just want to read a single article—although if you visit a newspaper's site regularly, you really should take the time to sign up because this helps the paper sell online ad space and stay in business.

I get a lot of my news from online news sites, which are updated all day long as new information comes in. Here are a few:

- CNN (www.cnn.com): The CNN TV news channel makes me tired because it's so darn busy! The CNN website, though, makes me happy because I can pick and choose the stories I want to follow.

- Google News (news.google.com): Search for news stories on any topic.

- Yahoo! News (news.yahoo.com): Get breaking news all day and search for stories of interest.

If you like your news in video form instead, check out YouTube News (www.youtube.com/news). What's especially interesting here is the News Near You feature, which displays news videos based on where you're signed in.

If you have trouble getting books back to the library in time to avoid fines, or if your local library is small or far away, you can use sites such as PaperBackSwap (www.paperbackswap.com) to exchange your used paperbacks with others. Illinois librarian Sarah J. explains, "PaperBackSwap is like having a giant used bookstore at your fingertips, and the only thing you pay is postage (usually less than $2.50) on outgoing books that other members request from you. In return, you get credits to use for requesting anything in the system. There is a wide selection, especially for bestsellers and romances. In the past 3 years, I've swapped over 250 books and saved over $1,100."

Booksfree (www.booksfree.com) is another option. This "Netflix for books" offers unlimited paperback rentals and prepaid shipping for a flat monthly fee, and you can choose from several different plans, ranging from two at a time to 15 at a time. Booksfree has similar plans for CD audiobooks for those who prefer to listen, as well as combo plans for those who do both.

Then there are ebooks, some of which you have to pay for, and some of which are free. The most well-known free ebook site, Project Gutenberg (www.gutenberg.org), contains thousands of free out-of-copyright titles for you to choose from and download. These are generally older titles. To find newer free ebooks, check sites like Amazon.com (of all places). Amazon.com often releases free ebooks for its Kindle ebook reader. To find these, visit the Kindle store on Amazon.com and sort by price, low to high, to bring the "zeros" (free ebooks) up first. Don't want to shell out the money for a Kindle? Me either, but you can download applications that let you read Kindle titles on both PCs and iPhones, with Mac and BlackBerry versions coming soon (www.amazon.com/gp/help/customer/display.html ?nodeId=200127470). Amazon.com also has some free PDF-format ebooks that you can read on your computer or mobile device. From the books section, choose "PDF" from the left-hand menu, and then again sort by price, low to high. Barnes & Noble has recently come out with its own ebook reader (www.barnesandnoble.com/ebooks/index.asp) for computers and mobile devices, which comes with some sample ebooks. It may release regular free samples, a la Amazon, as time goes on.

If, like me, you're a busy mom who never has enough time to read, you might also check out DailyLit (dailylit.com). This site sends short daily book installments via email or RSS. Read these on your computer or on your cell phone (this is a great way to keep busy in a waiting room or at soccer practice). Lastly, keep an eye out for free ebook announcements on the deal blogs you follow. Publishers and authors often release limited-time-only versions that you can grab to read at your leisure.

LISTEN TO IT ONLINE

Yes, there really are *legitimate* free and low-cost ways to listen to and download great music online. For one thing, don't pay a monthly fee for XM radio. Instead, use free services online that tailor their music to your listening tastes! Start by creating an account at Pandora internet radio (www.pandora.com). Pandora asks you to input artists or songs you like, then creates customized radio stations based on your own tastes. You can create multiple stations (currently up to 100) for multiple moods. You can give a thumbs-up to any songs they play that you love and a thumbs-down to those that miss the mark. And you will discover new songs and artists that are similar to those you already love. Over time, Pandora becomes more and more attuned to your personal likes and dislikes. Pandora is also available for BlackBerry, iPhone, and Windows mobile devices (pandora. com/#/extras/mobile-and-home), so you can listen anywhere you happen to be!

Last.fm (last.fm) also recommends music on the basis of artists you like. You can listen to built-in radio stations based around individual artists (Prince radio, Beatles radio, Johnny Cash radio) or genres (reggae, hard rock), listen to a station made up of tracks Last.fm recommends based on

Pandora

your previous listening habits, or listen to tracks you've added to your personal library. Last.fm includes music videos, photos, charts, and tons of other music-related resources. You can also download a free Last.fm application for your iPhone that allows you to listen while out and about. (Search for Last.fm or look in the music category of the app store on your phone.)

Beyond free radio, I like to look for free music downloads. This allows me to check out new music and artists, fill out my collection, have more to listen to while spending time online, and load songs onto my iPhone. Amazon.com regularly offers free album samplers and songs in various genres, individual artists and bands often release a sample song on their own websites, and some artists have even gone so far as to release entire albums for free download. Look up your favorite artists' websites to see what they have to offer and try the samplers to find new music. Here are some places to check for free music downloads:

- Amazon.com (www.amazon.com/Free-Songs-Music/b?ie=
  UTF8&node=334897011): Find a number of free MP3s for
  download; you can also sort by genre using the menu on the left.

- Amazon.com MP3 download newsletter (www.amazon.com/gp/
  gss/detail/841000): Sign up for weekly emails from Amazon.com
  that include info on new releases, hits, deals, and free samples.

- Last.fm (www.last.fm/music/+free-music-downloads): Find a
  constantly changing selection of free music downloads here from
  popular artists. Use the menu at the left to select a genre or just
  browse through the list.

- Walmart (instoresnow.walmart.com/In-Stores-Now-music-
  downloads.aspx): Find a new song for free download every week.

Free Music Downloads on Last.fm

All

acoustic

ambient

blues

classical

country

electronic

emo

folk

hardcore

hip hop

indie

jazz

latin

metal

pop

pop punk

punk

reggae

rnb

rock

soul

world

60s

70s

80s

90s

All MP3 Downloads

Dance Dance Dance (3:42)
Lykke Li
female vocalists, indie, swedish, pop, sweet
650,197 plays (145,106 listeners)
⬇ Free MP3

Shot In The Back Of The Head (3:14)
Moby
electronic, ambient, instrumental, moby, experimental
188,853 plays (46,608 listeners)
⬇ Free MP3

Discipline (4:18)
Nine Inch Nails
industrial, industrial rock, rock, electronic, alternative
939,889 plays (146,802 listeners)
⬇ Free MP3

Bear (3:53)
The Antlers
awesome, haunting, stunning, beautiful, ny
49,581 plays (12,657 listeners)
⬇ Free MP3

Space and the Woods (3:57)
Late of the Pier
new rave, electronic, electro, dance, electronica
511,021 plays (106,076 listeners)
⬇ Free MP3

The Start of Something (4:30)
Voxtrot
indie, indie pop, voxtrot, indie rock, catchy
652,781 plays (109,343 listeners)
⬇ Free MP3

Quand Tu Dors (3:50)
Aurélien Duval
french, chillout, pop, compositeur, france
28,039 plays (20,567 listeners)
⬇ Free MP3

Free music downloads on Last.fm

And as always, watch the deal blogs you follow for announcements of free downloadable songs and albums.

If you want to fill out your collection beyond what's available for free, iTunes and Amazon.com both offer music downloads for 99 cents to $1.29 a pop. Why not just buy and download your favorite tracks rather than shelling out for an entire CD?

Beyond music, you can also get your news radio online. NPR, for one, offers a free 24-hour stream at its website (www.npr.org). If you're spending a lot of time at the computer, you can keep up with current events at the same time. If you're looking for workout music, check out Motion Traxx (motiontraxx.com) for free dance-beat podcasts for runners and other types of aerobic exercisers.

WATCH IT ONLINE

Have you read any recent articles with advice from personal finance experts? One of the first things they advise is to cut back on nonessentials, such as that monthly cable bill or at least those premium channels. These seem like painful measures for a lot of us, especially when we're already cutting back on more expensive forms of entertainment. New online offerings, though, make the option more doable for many families.

First, take advantage of the new over-the-air digital television (DTV) offerings. This isn't like the old-time rabbit ears and tinfoil! With DTV, the picture quality is good and channels are plentiful. In addition to the major networks, there are a number of over-the-air specialty channels you can receive as well. The closer you live to a major city, the more channels you'll see. Check out AntennaWeb (antennaweb.org/aw/address.aspx) for a list of channels you might be able to receive in your area and find out much more about DTV at CancelCable.com (www.cancelcable.com).

To take advantage of DTV, you need a TV with a digital tuner (TVs purchased after March 2008 should have one built in) or a converter box (these run around $50; find places to buy them at www.dtv2009.gov). You will also need a roof or attic antenna, as well as a signal amplifier if you want to try to pull in extra channels. All of this, though, is a one-time investment that can then save you hundreds of dollars or more each year on that monthly cable or satellite TV bill.

You can also watch many of your shows online. A number of network sites now offer free advertiser-supported viewing of new shows online, often as early as the day after the original broadcast. Other sites offer pay-per-view movies or shows from premium channels such as HBO or Showtime. Compare costs here: If you're paying a monthly fee for cable *and* for a premium package just to watch a show or two on HBO or Showtime, you'll probably save quite a bit of money each month by just purchasing the individual episodes of the shows you want on iTunes or Amazon. You'll save even more in the off-season, when it's all reruns anyway! Check out these sites—some offer free streams of shows, others offer pay-per-view, and some help you locate your options for watching specific shows across the web. You'll need a high-speed internet connection to take advantage:

- Amazon.com Video On Demand (www.amazon.com/ gp/video/ontv/start): Have movies and shows sent to your TiVo or Roku box to watch on your TV instead of your PC (find out more at www.amazon.com/gp/video/ontv/ontv). It offers a mix of free and pay video; just click "Free Videos" to find out what you can watch for free. With TV shows, you can purchase individual episodes or a season pass that gives you a reduced per-episode price.

- CancelCable.com Showfinder (www.cancelcable. com/db/showfinder.php): Find places to watch all your favorite shows online.

- Clicker (www.clicker.com): Search or browse alphabetically or by category to find both free and pay shows from a number of websites.

- Fancast.com (www.fancast.com): Watch TV episodes and movies. Fancast offers a mix of free and pay-per-view titles, as well as access to Comcast on Demand.

- Hulu (www.hulu.com): Watch your favorite TV shows on demand—for free—at Hulu.

- iTunes (itunes.com): Purchase or rent movies and show episodes through iTunes.

Also visit the sites of the various networks you enjoy to see what shows they make available. Some let you watch new shows online for free as early as the morning after they broadcast.

Now let's talk DVDs. Are you still paying for DVDs, or are you renting new titles at $4.50 a pop at your local video store? Stop and think about your alternatives. The first, and cheapest, is to check out DVDs at your local public library. As long as you return them on time, borrowing them usually costs nothing, and larger library systems now have extensive collections. The downside is that you'll have to get on a waiting list for the newest and most popular materials, but you can put a number of things on your hold list and supplement your library viewing with some other strategies. If you don't have to watch a DVD the day it comes out, the library is for you.

Then look at Netflix (netflix.com). Besides the DVDs you can get through its monthly subscription plans, the "watch it now" option on Netflix offers another way to supplement your DVD and TV viewing. Each monthly plan includes unlimited "watch it now" viewing, and although much of the instantly viewable content is older, there's enough there to

Search results for "colbert"...

Network	Show	Hulu	Other	Netflix	Itunes
Comedy Central	The Colbert Report	view			view

Search for "Colbert" on the CancelCable.com Showfinder

keep you busy for a long, long time. If you watch a lot of streaming video on Netflix, look into getting a Roku box (www.roku.com/netflixplayer). This $100 gadget attaches to your TV and lets you easily stream Netflix content right onto your TV screen. My family has one; it's easy to use, and the quality is great! Netflix offers several monthly plans with free prepaid returns. The biggest competitor of Netflix is Blockbuster (www.block buster.com), which comes with the added bonus of being able to exchange DVDs in store for free or discounted rentals, rather than having to mail them back.

Aside from these subscription services, have you seen those new movie kiosks at grocery stores, drugstores, big box retailers, and some McDonald's? There are several different varieties, but the most popular is Redbox (redbox.com), which rents popular DVDs for just $1 per day. Even better, Redbox regularly releases codes for free movie rentals, letting you supplement your free online and over-the-air television viewing with free DVD rentals. To find these codes, follow the Inside Redbox blog (www.insideredbox.com), which keeps you up to date on new codes, new releases, and other Redbox info, and create an account at Redbox.com to get a free rental code via text message on the first Monday of every month. You can also sign up for an email newsletter on the Inside Redbox site. Some smaller kiosk competitors to Redbox include Blockbuster Express (www.bbexpressweb.com) and DVDPlay (www.dvdplay.com), but they

all work pretty much the same way. See what's available near you by
going to each site and entering your ZIP code.

Then there's YouTube (youtube.com), with its crazy mix of commercial
and user-generated content. My 7-year-old will sit contentedly watching
old *America's Funniest Home Videos* and *Tom & Jerry* cartoons on
YouTube until I kick him off of the computer ... but YouTube offers plenty
for grownups, too. Among the things I enjoy on YouTube: music videos.
(Since MTV no longer actually plays these, you're better off online.)

If you feel you're not quite ready to take the plunge, try experimenting
a little. Call your cable company and put your service on "vacation hold."
Most companies will do this for a certain time, and you won't have to pay
the bill while your account is on vacation. Try using the alternatives for a
bit and then reinstate your service if you find it's not working for you. Or
downgrade to basic service for a bit, supplement with the online offerings,
and see what you really miss.

ENTERTAIN YOURSELF (AND YOUR KIDS) ONLINE

You may think that the internet is the ultimate time waster. But think about
this: Before you purchase video games, workbooks, or educational games,
investigate some free online alternatives. Why buy a CD-ROM when you
can play an online educational game that's just as good? Why buy a work-
book when your kids can do interactive worksheets online or print out
worksheets from the internet?

Also use the internet to purchase discounted tickets to live shows,
movies, and other entertainment online and to find free and low-cost community events. Whenever you want to go to an event, check to see if there
are discount codes or tickets available. Use Goldstar (tickets.goldstar.com)
to find half-price tickets to a number of events, get discount tickets to
Broadway Shows at TheaterMania.com (www.theatermania.com), and find
free advance movie screenings at Free Movie Screenings (freemovie

screenings.net). Several theater chains offer deeply discounted kid's movies one morning a week during summer break. For instance, AMC Theatres runs a summer movie camp (www.amctheatres.com/smc) with $1 kids' movies each Wednesday at 10 AM.

Take advantage of online local resources that keep you aware of what's going on in your community. Visit your village or city website and bookmark its community calendar. It often lists free and low-cost community events, classes, and festivals. Visit your local library's website and check out its calendar to find free classes, children's programs, and other events. Be sure to take advantage of your local library's summer reading program, which usually offers prizes, performers, and other incentives to keep kids reading over the summer. Check the library's website for details.

FOR THE KIDS

You have literally hundreds of educational sites to choose from, making it difficult to justify spending money on pricey CD-ROM games that might not sustain your kid's interest. Here are just a very few of my own favorite "edutainment" sites for kids:

- PBS Kids (pbskids.org): Play games and do activities featuring all your favorite PBS characters.

- Scholastic Family Playground (scholastic.com/parents/play): Read, play games with, and watch favorite characters like Clifford the Big Red Dog.

- Starfall.com (www.starfall.com): Best for preschoolers through early elementary school, Starfall.com builds from simple letter and sound recognition through beginning phonics to beginning readers. This is a huge and in-depth site, and my older son used to spend hours there—yes, he was an early reader!

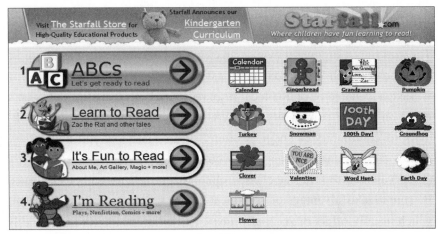

Starfall.com

If you do choose to invest in games on CD, make sure you're not buying something that can be done just as well online. If you've researched your purchase, though, some good places to look for games and educational software include:

- Amazon.com (www.amazon.com): Keep in mind that Amazon.com also allows third-party sellers to resell used products right alongside new ones, so you can often find gently used software at the site.

- Bird Rock Family Software (www.birdrockfamily.com): This site sells CDs at drastically discounted prices, the caveat being that these CDs usually come in a simple sleeve rather than complete with the entire boxed packaging. Be sure to sign up on the site to receive discount codes and sale notices via email.

- Garage sales and thrift stores: Younger kids, especially, won't mind if a game is "old" or if its graphics are somewhat outdated.

I've purchased CDs for as little as 10 cents at a garage sale—at that price, I don't care if they don't like it! If they don't, I can resell it at my own garage sale or add it to the Goodwill donation bag.

- Secondhand software and gaming stores.

For You

A bunch of gaming sites online let you play for free. Social networks such as Facebook offer third-party apps that let you play against your online "friends." Yahoo!'s games section (games.yahoo.com) offers downloadable games as well as interactive online games. For more online games than you'd ever want, you can also check out FOG (freeonlinegames.com), which offers Flash/Shockwave games that you play right in your internet browser.

Other places let you have fun by doing good. Check out sites such as FreeRice (www.freerice.com), which contains a progressively more challenging vocabulary game. For every correct answer, FreeRice donates 10 grains of rice through the U.N. World Food Program to Help End Hunger. (This is also a good vocabulary-building game for teenagers preparing for the SAT or ACT!)

Barter Goods and Services Online

A down economy can cause people to take a new look at bartering, or trading goods and services with each other. No money ever has to change hands! If your neighbor has a riding lawnmower and you love kids, why not swap babysitting for lawncare? If you have a mountain bike sitting in your garage that you never use anymore, maybe you could trade it for someone else's used laptop. Some neighbors use neighborhood email lists

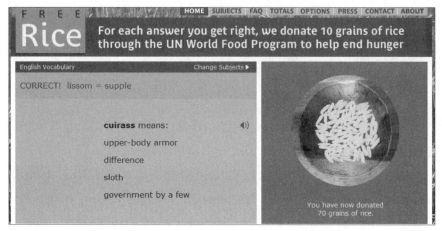

FreeRice

to track large items available for barter or sharing, and you can easily set up one of these at groups.yahoo.com.

Other online tools can also help you make these types of barter arrangements. craigslist (craigslist.com) is your main resource here. It has a Barter section under its For Sale classifieds, where you can post free ads or answer other people's ads. This can be a great way to get the goods and services you need—and get to know your neighbors at the same time. SwapThing (www.swapthing.com) does just what it says: It lets people swap "things" online. To help avoid shipping costs, you can limit your search to others in your local area. Trade A Favor (www.tradeafavor.com) works in a similar fashion. Finally, if you have a home or small business and are interested in bartering goods and services, check out the National Association of Trade Exchanges (NATE; www.nate.org) and International Trade Exchange (ITEX; www.itex.com).

FIND TRANSPORTATION OPTIONS ONLINE

Fuel prices bob up and down, but the general direction, unfortunately, is trending toward ridiculously high. This can inspire you to find money-saving alternatives to driving or to car ownership, or at least to find ways to economize or improve your gas mileage. Get all the info you need online. At the minimum, start with GasBuddy.com (www.gasbuddy.com) to compare current prices at local gas stations, which can vary tremendously. (You can also report local gas prices to help out others, earn points, and win prizes!) If you or anyone else in your family has to drive a lot, check out the list of the best cash-back-for-gas-purchase credit cards at PumpAndSave.com (www.pumpandsave.com).

Interested in car sharing? If you live in a major city, this is a viable option. Check out Zipcar (www.zipcar.com), which claims that its members save more than $500 each month (compared with the average cost of owning and operating a car in an urban environment). Save on parking, insurance, maintenance, and more when you use Zipcar on an as-needed basis. U-haul runs a similar U Car Share program (www.ucarshare.com/secure/Home.aspx) but only in a few cities so far. You can also look into ride-sharing options at Woodala (www.woodala.com), where people post ads looking for others to share rides and split gas costs, driving duties, and so on. Other ride-share sites to check out are eRideShare (erideshare.com) and GoLoco (www.goloco.org); craigslist also includes ride-share ads under its Community section. These sites are also useful in cities that have special high-occupancy-vehicle (HOV) lanes for cars with multiple occupants.

If you don't drive, Google Transit (www.google.com/transit) offers a user-friendly guide to mass transit in a number of cities. You can also use this resource to get transit directions on your mobile phone if you're out and about in a strange city.

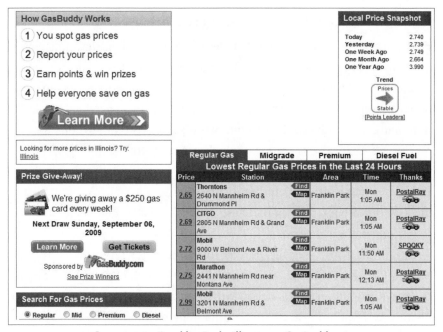

Gas prices in Franklin Park, Illinois, at GasBuddy.com

When it comes to flying the friendly skies, the internet has largely put an end to purchasing airline and hotel tickets through travel agents. Big-name sites such as Orbitz (orbitz.com), Travelocity (travelocity.com), and Expedia (expedia.com) have now cornered most of the market. Discount sites can also help you find air travel and hotel deals—although their fares are often last-minute or nondirect, so your plans might have to be flexible. Sites to look into here include:

- Airfarewatchdog (www.airfarewatchdog.com)

- Hotwire (hotwire.com)

- Last Minute Travel (www.lastminutetravel.com)

- Priceline (priceline.com)

- SunTrips (suntrips.com)

- Travelzoo (travelzoo.com)

These sites also often let you sign up to get alerts on fare deals through email, again letting info come to you!

As always, don't stick with just one site. Look around to see which one has the best deal, especially on a high-cost item such as airline tickets. Sites like BookingBuddy (www.bookingbuddy.com) and Cheapflights (www. cheapflights.com) search multiple travel sites at once to find the best fare. And, for when you get there, search Hotels.com (www.hotels.com), which sometimes has better rates than even a hotel's own site.

Don't let the ideas in this chapter limit you. Find discounts or alternatives for almost anything you can think of, all online. These are just a few examples of what's out there when you start poking around the World Wide Web.

6

Fantastic Freebies

I've already talked about the fact that when you embark on your frugal journey, your family may come along only grudgingly. One way to help combat their frustration is to take advantage of free samples, in-home product testing opportunities, and similar offers to treat yourself and the rest of the family with unexpected surprises. This is another way to help avoid the sense of deprivation that can come from any lifestyle adjustment that involves saving more and spending less. Besides, it's kind of *fun* to see what random samples might come in the mail during any given week. In the past month alone, I've received granola bars, (plastic) shot glasses, posters, cereal, paper towels, tote bags, deodorant, shampoo, toothpaste, coupons, magazine subscriptions … and more!

While I wouldn't necessarily have paid money for every single one of these items in a store, I'll surely try them for free, and I sometimes have found unexpected delights. Companies send out freebies for the same reason they give out in-store samples: They want to convert you to purchasing and using their products, so give them a fair shake. If you like a product you sample, you might go out and buy it in the future. (And these samples often come with coupons to sweeten the deal!)

In this chapter, learn how to find online offers for freebies that make checking your mailbox fun.

FREEBIE SITES

Every Friday, I do a freebie roundup at MashupMom.com, and other bargain bloggers often post freebies either as a weekly roundup or as they come across them. Once you find your own mix of blogs to follow, you'll find many different freebies to send away for!

You can also check out sites and blogs that focus largely or entirely on freebies. Here are a few to get you started:

- Free Sample Freak (freesamplefreak.com): Read this blog devoted entirely to freebies.

- Free Stuff Times (www.freestufftimes.com): Find legitimate freebie offers, updated throughout the day.

- FreeStuff4Free.com (www.freestuff4free.com): Check out the newest freebie offers on the front page or browse the categories in the menu on the left.

- Freebies 4 Mom (freebies4mom.com): Look for freebies and links to printable coupons and other money-saving info.

- Freebies for Individuals (www.hotcouponworld.com/forums/ freebies-individuals): Check this forum where members post information about the freebies they find.

- Hey, It's Free! (www.heyitsfree.net): Find several freebies— with attitude—daily.

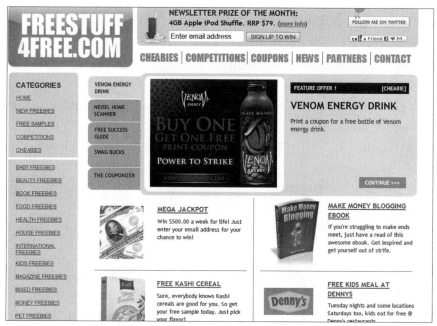

FreeStuff4Free.com

- Walmart (instoresnow.walmart.com/In-Stores-Now-Free-Samples.aspx): Check weekly or so to see what's new on Walmart's site, where it regularly offers free samples. (Note that at this writing, the site doesn't work well in Firefox, so you may want to use Internet Explorer.)

When you're browsing any site, watch out for anything that asks you to complete an offer to get a freebie. If you have to buy something, it's not really free, is it? Watch out also for sites that don't "feel" right. If it seems too good to be true, it just might be.

WORD-OF-MOUTH MARKETING PROGRAMS

Companies and marketing agencies have caught on to the power of the internet as a huge word-of-mouth marketing resource. We all know that people are more likely to trust a friend's or a colleague's opinion over a company's professionally produced marketing materials. Word-of-mouth marketing programs put companies' new or improved products into your hands so that you can talk them up, review them online, and share your opinions with others. This is doubly neat: You get a product to try out, and your opinions and recommendations can help influence companies' products and decisions.

Here are some word-of-mouth marketing sites you might want to look into:

- BzzAgent (www.bzzagent.com): BzzAgent works with a lot of different companies to create "bzz" around their new or changed products. Sign up on the site for bzz products and services. Your survey answers, participation on the site, and reports on your campaigns work together to get you more invitations to new campaigns. When you are invited into a campaign and accept that invitation, BzzAgent will send you the product (or a coupon to get it for free at the store), coupons for your friends, and information to help you talk up the product to others. You'll need to visit the BzzAgent site regularly to report back on your conversations with others about these products. The more active you are on the BzzAgent site, the greater chance you have of being invited to join one of these product campaigns.

- House Party (www.houseparty.com): House Party works with brands to sponsor parties in consumers' homes across the country. When you sign up, you'll receive emails about upcoming parties and have the chance to qualify for each. If you get into one of these campaigns, House Party will mail you a party pack containing enough products to share with all of your friends at a party you host at your home.

- Kraft First Taste (www.kraftfirsttaste.com): Kraft Foods lets consumers sign up for a chance to try out its new products on an occasional basis and then share their opinions in polls and with friends. Participants can also share coupons for these products by entering their friends' email addresses on the site.

- ModernMom.com (www.modernmom.com): This online community for moms sometimes offers members the chance to try out new products.

- Mom Central (www.momcentral.com/go/mom/testing): Sign up for its Mom Testing Panel for opportunities to test products and services, take online surveys, and otherwise provide your opinion.

- One2One Network (www.one2onenetwork.com): Women from 21 to 70-plus are invited to give feedback on sample products, get samples or coupons to share with their friends, throw themed house parties featuring products, and participate in online viral marketing campaigns.

- Pssst... (pssst.generalmills.com): General Mills provides members with news about new products, as well as occasional samples and coupons. It also lets members share printable and mailed coupons with friends. (As I was writing this chapter, for instance, I received an envelope from Pssst... with a coupon for *free* 50-calorie Fiber One yogurt, plus a set of other Fiber One yogurt coupons. Of course I'm going to try it and talk about it. See? I just did!)

- SheSpeaks (www.shespeaks.com): Women can sign up to test products and provide reviews.

- Smile.ly (smile.ly): Try new products and share your thoughts.

- Tryology (www.expotv.com/make/tryology): This site gives you the opportunity to try and review new products, but you must be willing and able to create a *video* review and upload it to the site.

- Vocalpoint (www.vocalpoint.com): Besides mailing product samples, Vocalpoint, created by Procter & Gamble, often mails or emails high-value coupons.

These word-of-mouth marketing sites emphasize that they are *not* "freebie" sites. In other words, they're not just giving you a random gift or sample: By accepting the products they send, you also accept the responsibility for reviewing the product, discussing it, or promoting it to your friends and colleagues. These sites will often give you "talking points" to use in these conversations, as well as coupons for the products to hand out to others. If you're uncomfortable with these obligations, it's best not to sign up.

Some sites ask that users come back to answer online surveys about their experience with a product or to post reviews of the product. Remember to be honest. Realize that you're part of an extended online focus group and that companies will use your feedback to improve or tweak their products. If you didn't like the product, say so and tell them why not. If you loved it, tell them that, too. It's exciting to know that your opinions can help shape a company's products!

MAGAZINE SUBSCRIPTIONS

There's a magazine published for every interest, and you can often snag free subscriptions to these online as well. Some of these are niche publications (for everyone from horse lovers to website designers), and some are

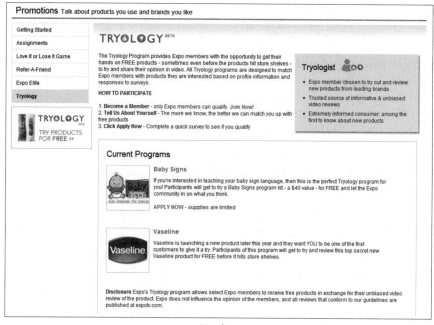

Tryology

more general consumer magazines. Sites that often offer magazine sub-scriptions include:

- FreeBizMag.com (www.freebizmag.com): While this site pur-ports to offer free *business* publications, it often offers general consumer magazines as well. The catch? You need to sign up on the site and then answer questionnaires to "qualify" for each magazine offer.

- Mercury Magazines (www.mercurymagazines.com): Mercury Magazines also says it's a site for free "business publications," but I have managed to get free subscriptions here to consumer magazines such as *O: The Oprah Magazine.*

- StartSampling (www.startsampling.com): Beyond its usual free product samples, Start Sampling often offers free magazine subscriptions to members.

- ValueMags (www.valuemags.com/home/index.asp): This site sells magazine subscriptions but also offers freebies fairly often.

A number of blogs, including mine, do regular roundups or posts about new magazine subscription offers, so you needn't remember to keep visiting these magazine sites to try to find them. Free subscription offers pop up on a seemingly random basis and are usually limited in time and scope. Once a certain number of people sign up or the signup date has passed, the offer disappears. So you need to watch for them and subscribe to magazines of interest as they appear. (Some popular magazine subscription offers last only *hours*!)

Why would anyone give away magazines for free? On the face of it, this doesn't seem right. After all, it's not like a free sample, where the company is trying to entice you to buy its product. Here, you're simply *getting* the product—the magazine—for free! Here's the deal: Most consumer magazines don't make their money on subscriptions. They make it on *advertising*. The more subscribers they have, the better they look to advertisers. The better they look to advertisers, the more ads they can sell, and the more they can charge for these ads. So, relax. You're doing them a favor by subscribing, even if you're not paying for that subscription.

Keep in mind that a lot of magazines also contain coupons. This occasionally includes magazines where you might not expect to find coupons. Just last summer, for instance, *Maxim* and *Men's Fitness* magazines—both of which were available for free a couple months earlier—contained coupons for free Axe products. About the same time, several grocery chains across the country were offering customers free movie tickets for buying a certain number of Axe products. Talk about win-win! Get a free magazine, use the coupon in it to buy a free product, and get a free movie ticket! This is another reason to subscribe when these free offers roll around; you never know what extra savings they'll offer you.

BIRTHDAY FREEBIES

Get a birthday present from the internet! A number of restaurants and other companies run online birthday clubs. When you sign up on these websites, coupons and other offers will be mailed or emailed to you during your birthday month, and some of these offers, such as entirely free restaurant meals, are pretty good. (Free food that I don't have to cook equals a happy mom!) Take advantage and have a date night—or two—to celebrate your birthday. Some places will also email you coupons for a free appetizer, a buy-one-get-one-free entrée, or a free dessert, just for joining.

Here are a just few of these clubs to get you started. Sign yourself up as well as your husband or significant other; some of these clubs will give you coupons for anniversaries as well. Most chain restaurants offer some sort of a birthday club or loyalty program, so check with your favorites to see what they have going:

- Baskin Robbins (www.baskinrobbins.com/bdayclub/ RegisterInfo1.aspx): Get a free scoop!

- Benihana (www.benihana.com/email): Get a coupon for a free birthday dinner (up to $30) each year.

- Cold Stone Creamery (www.coldstonecreamery.com/Birthday/ birthday_club.aspx): Get a free "creation" for your birthday.

- Famous Dave's (www.famousdaves.com/pig-club): Sign up for its P.I.G. (Pretty Important Guest) club, and you'll get a coupon for anything from a free dessert to a free family feast every year.

- The Melting Pot (www.themeltingpotclubfondue.com): Get free chocolate fondue for two when you sign up—and on your birthday!

- Noodles & Company (noodle.fbmta.com/members/UpdateProfile. aspx?Action=Subscribe): Get a printable emailed coupon for a free meal in your birthday month each year.

Also sign up for birthday and restaurant clubs for your kids. You will need to do this for children under 13, who can't sign themselves up for marketing offers online. Here are a few legitimate and fun options:

- Burger King (www.clubbk.com/Parents): Register kids 12 and under for a free hamburger meal near their birthday.

- California Pizza Kitchen (www.cpk.com/cpkids): Sign up and kids 10 and under get a free kid's meal during their birthday month.

- The Children's Place (www.childrensplace.com/webapp/ wcs/stores/servlet/birthday_10001_10001_-1): Get something that's more for *you*—a 20-percent-off coupon in your child's birthday month!

- Denny's (www.dennys.com/LiveImages/enProductImage_ 334.pdf): Fax or mail in this form, and your children (10 and under) will receive a card good for a free kid's entrée and sundae for their birthday.

- Shoney's Kids Club (www.shoneys.com/kids-club-signup.html): Get free birthday kid's meal and "other surprises throughout the year" for kids 10 and younger.

- Toys R Us (www.birthdaysrus.com/grownups): Join this club for ages 1 through 10, and Toys R Us mails a $3 coupon good toward anything in the store a month before each child's birthday—plus a postcard your child can bring into the store for a birthday crown or balloon.

Remember, I'm just listing a very few here to give you an idea of what's available. You can find a long, long list of birthday clubs to join at FreeBirthdayTreats.com (www.freebirthdaytreats.com). Check with your favorite local restaurants, too—non-chain restaurants might not make it onto these birthday lists but often have great offerings for kids (and grownups).

RESTAURANT FREEBIES

Beyond birthday freebies, some restaurants offer occasional or annual freebie events. When you sign up for their eclubs, they'll keep you informed about these via email as well. A few regular offerings:

- Ben & Jerry's (www.benjerry.com/scoop-shops/feature/free-cone-day): Every April, Ben & Jerry's runs a free cone day at participating ice cream shops. (Another great one for the kids!)

- IHOP (www.ihoppancakeday.com): Every customer gets a free short stack of pancakes on national pancake day. Donations to the Children's Miracle Network are requested but optional.

- IKEA (info.ikea-usa.com/seizethedays): IKEA offers a free small breakfast and coffee during an entire weekend every 6 to 8 weeks or so and offers free kids' meals on occasion as well. Check the website or local ads to find out when it's running this deal.

Some restaurants also let kids eat free (with purchase of an adult meal) on certain days of the week. If you're planning on taking the family out to dinner, try to do so during one of these offerings. You can save quite a bit on kids' meals, which, as you probably know by now, can be crazy expensive.

To find these deals, check out KidsMealDeals (kidsmealdeals.com). Just put in your ZIP code to find which restaurants offer free kids' meals, on which days of the week, and with what purchase requirements (usually up to two free kids' meals with purchase of an adult entrée). This site works best with national chains, so ask local restaurants whether they have similar offerings.

SURVEY SITES

You'll find more about survey sites as money-making opportunities in Chapter 8, and I'll list some specific ones to try there. Here, I just want to mention that these sites often seek consumers to test actual products in their homes and report on their experiences. I've personally tested and then given my feedback on products from baby wipes to shampoo and conditioner. You might take a number of surveys before you run across one whose sponsor asks you to test an actual product, but it does happen on a fairly regular basis. Be willing to give your honest feedback and to use the product according to the survey site's instructions. They're looking for opinions from real-life consumers. That's you!

SWEEPSTAKES AND GIVEAWAYS

Another way companies try to build brand loyalty is by offering online sweepstakes, most of which you can enter for free, even if you haven't purchased the product. This is something that's fun to do if you have a few spare minutes. In many sweepstakes, you have pretty good odds of at least winning small prizes, such as product coupons. It may sound like I'm advising you to play the lottery, but just to be clear, I'm not! The difference is that all it costs you to play is your time. Check sites such as Sweeties Sweepstakes (www.sweetiessweeps.com), which talks about the most "winnable" sweepstakes, offers links to them, and gives you tips on maximizing your chances of winning. Sweepstakes Advantage (www.sweepsadvantage.com) is another site to try if you're looking for online sweepstakes to enter. If you want to combine sweepstakes and surveys, you can sign up for Instant Cash Sweepstakes (www.instantcash sweepstakes.com). Take fun three-question surveys each day for the chance to win cash, paid out via PayPal.

On blogs, the odds of winning sweepstakes and giveaways are *much* better than in the big national sweepstakes. Blog contests tend to receive just tens or hundreds of entries, instead of hundreds of thousands as do the heavily advertised sweepstakes from major companies. Many major companies have started cashing in on the power of "mommy bloggers," who offer a built-in audience and the authenticity of an independent voice. Companies often offer some of their new products as giveaways for readers of high-traffic blogs. These opportunities will pop up on the deal blogs you follow, so be sure to take a minute to enter—you just might get lucky!

Some frugal bloggers host weekly roundups of new giveaways on other blogs. For instance, check out the Giveaway Gathering at Deal Seeking Mom (www.dealseekingmom.com/category/giveaway-gathering) and Want to Win Wednesday at Nickels-n-Dimes (blog.nickels-n-dimes.com/?cat=32). These roundups usually list literally hundreds of blog giveaways to enter, so why not give it a try?

LOCAL FREEBIE RESOURCES

You can find free local offers of other people's gently used items as well. First, sign up for your local Freecycle (www.freecycle.org) email list. Always keep in mind that Freecycle is technically *not* a "freebies" site. It's actually a grassroots network of people who give (and get) items locally for free, in order to keep perfectly usable things from ending up in landfills. Freecycle can be a great resource for picking up outgrown kids' clothes, baby toys, and other items you often find at garage sales. Members also often freecycle old technology, so if you're still relying on the library's computers and internet, this might be an avenue to locating an older but usable computer.

Visit Freecycle to locate a site near you, and then join its local Yahoo! Group to receive and post messages about available items. Most Freecycle groups have guidelines for members. For instance, users may need to make an "offer" of an unwanted item before they can request an item. When you join, you become part of the Freecycle community, so be sure to give, as well as receive.

Some alternatives to Freecycle include (the smaller) Freesources (www.freewebs.com/freesourcesnetwork), as well as the free sections of the classifieds on craigslist (www.craigslist.org; look in the "free" section under "for sale" on your local craigslist).

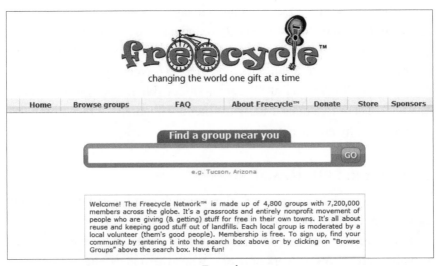

Freecycle

SMOOTHING OUT THE KINKS

Here are just a few words of advice to help your online freebie-gathering experience run more smoothly:

1. Request only freebies you are actually interested in. If you are just going to throw something away, don't waste your time filling out a form or waste the company's money and effort in sending it to you.

2. Request only freebies that seem legitimate. Avoid requesting freebies from sites that seem amateurish or that don't seem connected to a company in any other way; some of these are just scams, set up to collect information in order to send spam. (It helps to stick to freebies found through bloggers you trust, because they'll vet the links for you.)

3. Don't get disappointed if items don't arrive. Sometimes freebies are advertised but don't actually show up. Think of freebies as a bonus, and remember that those from large, reputable companies are more likely to arrive.

4. Use a free program such as RoboForm (www.roboform.com/download.html) to automate the process of filling out lengthy forms online. (RoboForm offers a "free" and a "pro" version; free will be sufficient for most people's needs.)

5. Get one of those free email accounts (see Chapter 1) and use it whenever you sign up online for freebies. Many sample offers require that you sign up for an online newsletter or otherwise get on a "list," and you don't want all of this cluttering up your main email account. Also, if you do get caught by one of the less-than-legitimate spam offers, you don't want the junk mail going to your personal account.

6. Realize that sites ask for personal information such as your birth date because they are required to do so by U.S. law, which prevents them from collecting personal information from children 13 or younger for the purposes of marketing to them. You might also get a coupon or other surprise on your birthday!

7. If you're uncomfortable giving out a piece of personal information, leave it blank (if the form lets you) or realize that the only one who knows whether this is your real phone number is you!

Now what do you do with all these freebies? Aside from using them, donating them, or selling them at a garage sale, here are some ideas:

TOILETRIES AND OTC MEDICINE

- Create travel bags with sample-sized toiletries. These are particularly handy when you fly and have to comply with Transportation Security Administration regulations on the size and type of items you can bring aboard a plane. Throw the tiny toothpaste, deodorant, and shampoo you receive into a quart-sized Ziploc bag and call it a day.

- Put sample soap, shampoos, and so on into a pretty basket in a guest bathroom for guests who have forgotten their own toiletries.

- Donate them to the troops!

FOOD

- Give it to the kids. Let them sample the "fun" food items you get for free, which also helps them get on that frugality bandwagon.

Throw a free granola bar in their lunchbox; pop up some free popcorn after school.

- Use it to help guide your shopping decisions. Would you pay for this product? Would you buy it again? How does your family like the product?

- Try items you wouldn't normally buy.

- Eat it!

MAGAZINES

- Read them, then pass them along to friends—or start a magazine swap!

- Leave copies in public locations (tear your address info from the cover first) so that people in airports and waiting rooms have some free reading material too.

- Sell them at a garage sale.

- Donate them to your local library's book and magazine sale.

- Sell them to a used bookstore—some stores also buy used magazines or will give you store credit for these. (Even if you get only 10 cents an issue or store credit, you've gotten them for free, read them, and now can benefit further!)

- Give them away on Freecycle.

Above all, have fun—and enjoy the surprises!

7

Make Money at Home

Now that I've told you all my favorite ways to save—which can, of course, be a job in itself—let's talk about the other side of the equation: *making* money from home. Here, as always, think about what will be the right balance for you. You might find that saving money on groceries and other everyday purchases is enough for your family. Or you might want to bring in a little on the side for fun things, Christmas, or extras. Or you might want to go all out and find a part- or full-time job. (The next chapter talks more about ways to make a little side money with your everyday online activities.) Me, I do a mix of everything. I freelance, I answer surveys online, I blog—the more options you can mash up, the better! And the more fun.

You can also use online resources in just about *any* home business, whether you advertise your home day care on craigslist, email a regular newsletter to clients, create Facebook events for your direct sales business, or write a regular column on someone else's website. It's hard to launch a home business these days without some sort of an online presence.

But it's also hard to figure out how to use online resources to find legitimate ways to make money from home, how to avoid scams, and how to pick the right option or options for you. So here are a number of ways to make money with the use of online resources, ranging from selling on eBay or Etsy to using your existing skills to launch a home business. Keep in mind that most of these ideas offer a nice *side* income but won't replace a full-time job. (There's just no easy way to get rich quick online!) You can use the internet in other ways, too, to market a business, communicate with customers, and network with other freelancers and at-home workers.

This chapter mentions only a few work-at-home options to help get you thinking about the possibilities. Think about your own skills and where you might fill a need—you might find that you can do something totally different! For more ideas on ways to make money from home, listen to some of the podcasts at Frugal WAHMs Talk Radio (frugalwahmstalkradio.com) and check out Women For Hire's work-at-home section (www.women forhire.com/work_from_home).

This chapter does not talk about all the nuts and bolts (and taxes!) involved in setting up a home business. But you do need to be aware that jumping into self-employment means that you'll need to deal with a lot of details that your former employer took care of in the past: taxes, budgeting, accounting, marketing. You can find many useful resources to help you down that road when you're ready to take that step. Check out Nolo's (www.nolo.com) consulting and contracting center and its many books on the legal aspects of self-employment and freelancing. Your local library should also have books and resources on starting a home business and dealing with the tax and legal issues involved, which can vary from state to state.

Lastly, realize that working at home really is *work* and that it may take some time to see results from your time and effort. Stick with it and see what happens!

eBay, Etsy, and Effortless Online Selling

OK, selling online may not be exactly *effortless*. But over the past few years, as more people have gone online and obtained high-speed internet access, there has been an explosion in the popularity of online auction and shopping sites. These allow you to reach many more people than you could through a garage sale or local craft fair. And sites that focus on a particular niche allow you to focus on what best fits your own mix of skills.

If you don't want to *sell* online, try something new: Rent your items on a site like Zilok (zilok.com). You can offer things for rent through this site and collect payment directly from the local person who rents an item from you. Zilok takes a commission on each rental.

Amazon.com

Like books? Amazon.com offers a Marketplace program (sellercentral. amazon.com) in which third-party listings of used items such as books, videos, and CDs show up right on the same page as the listing for a new title. This offers Marketplace sellers a fantastic advantage in reaching users on the hugely popular Amazon.com site. Amazon.com doesn't charge a fee to list items, but when items do sell, it deducts a commission of 6 percent to 15 percent of the sales price, a per-transaction fee of 99 cents, and a variable closing fee. Amazon.com also charges Marketplace buyers a flat $3.99 fee for media mail shipping, which it passes on to you; on most items, you'll make something back on the shipping as well. (This is why some sellers list items as low as a penny—they're making a bit on the shipping on each sale.)

Amazon.com charges buyers' credit cards through its own infrastructure, then automatically disburses funds to sellers every 2 weeks via direct deposit to their checking accounts. Sellers must have a valid U.S. checking account and credit card to participate in the Amazon Marketplace program.

Where do you find books, CDs, and videos to resell on Amazon? Some of the best places include garage sales, thrift shops, and used book sales at your local library (although realize that library and other markings will detract from a book's condition and value). Over time, you will get a feeling for the types of items that are more likely to sell. Manda C., a Minneapolis 30-something, sells "used books on Amazon.com to make money from home. I find them cheap at thrift stores and garage sales, and resell them for a small profit. It's not a whole lot, but it's a step toward my goal of having a telecommuting or a flex job once I have a family." Selling online on Amazon, eBay, or elsewhere can be a great alternative to selling-at-home parties and other popular ways of earning money from home. Manda C. continues, "I want a job doing something, not soliciting my friends and family to buy stuff. There's a place for that, and these vendors do provide a service for very outgoing people that need an outlet, but I'm an introvert. I'd lose electricity and not put food on the table being responsible for selling stuff on my personality alone."

You can see that this is really a volume business—you won't make a lot of money unless you sell hundreds of items each month. However, if you are already making the thrift store and garage sale rounds to find items to sell on eBay, you might supplement your eBay sales with book and other media sales on Amazon.com. While you *can* sell books on eBay, they tend to do better on Amazon.com because of its heavyweight status in the online book-selling arena. When selling online, you can think about using multiple sites and listing only the types of items on each that tend to do best.

CafePress

Remember those T-shirt shops you used to find in malls, where you could create your own slogans or choose from hundreds of designs? These have moved online, and CafePress (www.cafepress.com) allows anyone to set up shop and sell T-shirts, mugs, mousepads, and anything else you can slap a graphic, slogan, or logo onto. If you have a clever, unique, or just plain funny idea, get yourself a CafePress store. It costs nothing to set up, and you'll earn a commission on each item sold.

CRAIGSLIST

The giant online classifieds site craigslist (craigslist.com) provides a different option for those wanting to sell items locally. This is a great service for unloading bulkier items you might not want to ship, and it's always free to post an ad (unless you are posting in the "adult" section). Free classifieds are a big plus over sites such as eBay, which charge a listing fee and then take a percentage of every purchase.

The downside of craigslist, though, is that, as simply an online classifieds system, it lacks the seller protections provided by sites such as Amazon.com and eBay. You'll also need to work out payment methods with buyers, as well as a way to get the item to them. Do you want people to come to your home to pick up items, or do you want to deliver or ship them or meet buyers at a neutral location? If you're selling only smaller, lower-cost items, it might not be worth the hassle to arrange payment and pickup with buyers. Take some time to browse the ads on your local craigslist to get an idea of the types of items people sell and think about supplementing your other online sales by using this site.

EBAY

As with Amazon.com, eBay (ebay.com) is really a volume business. If you're selling lower-priced items (clothing, toys, collectables), you don't make a lot on each one, especially after eBay dings you at both ends (when you list and when you sell). You'll need to get a sense for what types of items are in demand and how to value your own time in locating items to sell.

If nothing else, selling on eBay or elsewhere can help you reduce clutter and organize your life! Many moms who resell on eBay also gather items at garage sales and thrift stores, supplementing these with what their own kids have outgrown. Items not selling? Think about donating them and claiming the tax deduction. Goodwill has a handy valuation guide online (www.goodwill.org/get-involved/donate/taxes-and-your-donation) that helps you value goods that you are donating to Goodwill or another charitable organization.

In Her Own Words

Tammy J. is an eBay reseller and a frugal mom of three.

I started selling on eBay in 2004, after my first son was born. I found it was an easy way to make a little extra money from home, selling things that I would be getting rid of anyway. I started selling clothing and shoes my son had outgrown and anything else around the house that I didn't need or want any longer. I saw how easy it was to make a little cash, and I haven't stopped!

I now find items to sell around my own home and also at thrift stores and yard or garage sales. I have three small children, and they are constantly outgrowing clothes, so I sell their clothes in "lots" on eBay. I find items discounted at the local thrift stores and yard sales to sell on eBay, such as children's clothing, women's jeans, etc., and I also sell coupons. I sell Sunday newspaper inserts in multiples, or I email several companies at a time and compliment a product I like. Often these companies will send coupons for free products, and I auction them in a lot on eBay.

These do very well. If I have 10 free product coupons, I can often sell these for $25 to $30—and this is just for an hour or less of emailing companies!

I do not specialize in a particular item, and I am still learning about great items to sell, but I do sell a lot of children's clothing and jeans. They seem to do very well, especially if they are in groups or lots of the same size and in good condition. I also use coupons and rebates and store promotions to get items free or close to free and then sell them on eBay! I do not currently run an eBay store. Since my time is very limited with three children, I do not feel that I could keep a store in stock at all times and prefer auction-style listings.

Nine times out of ten I start my auction at 99 cents. This seems to always attract people to an item and generate more bids. Many people seem to be hesitant to start an item at 99 cents because they are afraid they will not get the true value of an item. Sometimes this is true, and I have had items start and end at 99 cents, but most of the time that is not the case—I just sold a 25-piece lot of children's clothing for $104 and started them at 99 cents!

If it is an item I know to be pretty valuable and I think only a handful of people might be attracted to it, such as collectors, I will start it higher or offer a "Buy It Now." I have had auctions listed at 99 cents for which buyers email me and ask if I can add it as a Buy It Now auction, and I am always happy to do this. I just ask them to make an offer! I maximize the chances of selling an item by starting it at a low price, like 99 cents, adding as many pictures as possible (buyers love pictures), offering the lowest shipping possible or free shipping (also attracts attention to the auction), and advertising my listings. I don't do a lot of marketing for my eBay auctions, but I do belong to a forum that has a whole section about eBay, and I do list a link to my auctions there, especially if it's an item that I think will be of interest to that particular group of people.

I love being able to stay at home with my children and make money! I also was born a bargain hunter, so the "job" part of it is fun for me! I love looking through thrift stores and discount stores for products to sell, and I also love clothes, so I don't mind the handling and picture taking part of it either. I would definitely call this a part-time job—I try to go thrifting at least three times a week, and I list 30 to 40 auctions a week. I am hopeful that in the future I can make this a full-time job, but I have three small children and don't have the time to put in every single day. It can be very time-consuming.

If you're just getting started, take it slow at first and get a feel for eBay. Find out what items are popular, and if you have some things around the house that you no longer want or need, go ahead and list them and see what happens. You might be surprised! If you are thinking about doing this as a job, be aware that it is very time-consuming and you have to have a lot of self-discipline. Also, do a lot of research! Research eBay's completed listings and find websites that offer information on great items to sell. I have been selling casually for a long time, and while thrifting I have looked over a lot of items that I could have made a great profit on—but I didn't know enough. I recently have been doing a lot of research, and in about a month I have learned about many more items that I can look for while out that do very well on eBay. I belong to a forum that has a few work-at-home moms as members, but many of them are also casual eBay sellers, and we talk about our auctions and eBay experiences. I also have subscribed to the eBay Coach's blog, and I frequent it often for more ideas on items to sell.

I used to consider couponing my part-time job. I have saved so much money for my family by using coupons and bargain hunting. As my eBay business grows, it has been a little harder to balance them both. I try to set aside time for couponing and deal hunting after I have finished my eBay work for the day. Couponing is very important for me to keep my household in stock, and it also gives me another way to get inventory for eBay. Many items that I get for free with coupons I can sell on eBay!

I definitely think it is especially important now to save money and use coupons. As prices rise I cringe at the thought of paying full price for something, but luckily I never have to! As for eBay, I don't see a drastic change in my business. I see a lot more people trying to save money, so this can really help the eBay business. Everyone is looking for a bargain, so buying something on eBay secondhand may be saving some a lot of money. Also, it helps me sell coupons, because a lot more people seem to be using coupons to save money. They may go to eBay to buy them in lots or multiples to save some money and time.

ETSY

Are you crafty? Do you create handmade gifts for friends and family or to sell locally? Move beyond local craft fairs to get your work out to the entire world through Etsy (www.etsy.com), a huge online craft marketplace. The more unique and interesting your product, the better—think about a niche you can fill or a market you can reach.

Displaying your work on a site such as Etsy gives you advantages over trying to set up your own online store. You get the advantage of the Etsy name and people's ability to search on the site. Plus, the site takes care of the online payment part of things, leaving you free to design your creations. It's free to set up a store, but Etsy charges you 20 cents per item listing and a 3.5 percent commission on sales.

GARAGE SALES

While selling things at a garage sale is not selling online, many couponers find success in selling some of their bargains in yearly garage or yard sales. If you're able to buy things at pennies on the dollar, you can then sell those items to others at far below retail, while still making a profit. Surprisingly, stockpilers are able to sell everything from toothpaste to barbecue sauce at yard sales, clearing out their pantries while cleaning up on profit. And if you have used coupons to get snack food and pop on the cheap, let your kids set up a refreshment table at the sale and get them involved by letting them keep some of the earnings! This is another way to get your family on board with the whole saving and stockpiling idea.

When you stockpile items over the year with an eye toward a sale, you can focus on collecting as many free and nearly free items as possible, without worrying about whether your family will use these items. (For instance, buy dog treats that are free after coupon, even if you don't have a dog.) Just be sure you have a place to store your finds and that they won't expire before your sale.

Sati of CafeMom explains, "I just had a *huge* garage sale/stockpile sale, and I got $3,049 from it. Yes, you read that right—and I only sold about half my stockpile. I figure my total out-of-pocket cost on my whole stockpile to be about $600, including costs for the sale, so I made $2,449 on this sale. I plan on having another sale at the end of the summer, and should make another $1,500 then. So couponing for me *really* is a part-time job!"

While most garage salers aren't likely to clear thousands, the larger your stockpile and the more heavily trafficked your sale, the better your chance of success. Get the word out as widely as possible. Use craigslist, which offers free garage sale listings, but also consider putting an ad in your local classifieds section and getting large, brightly colored signs out on major intersections. If you can piggyback on a neighborhood garage sale, even better!

If you are also an eBayer, you can try selling items that haven't gone on eBay at your garage sale, as well as bulkier items you don't want to deal with the hassle of shipping. If an item doesn't sell at your garage sale, you can try selling it on craigslist. You'll find a different market everywhere, so you never know when the right person will come along for the right item!

When you're planning your sale and pricing items, you might want to check out a useful (and lengthy) thread on Slickdeals (tinyurl.com/mgfyva), in which stockpilers talk about how they priced items at their own garage sales, what sold, and what didn't. If you get ambitious about chasing bargains and have a *huge* stockpile to sell off, you can think about branching out and renting a table at local flea markets or community garage sales.

In Her Own Words

Kate I. is a mom of one and owner/designer of Brittain Road Designs.

My Etsy store is called Brittainroad.etsy.com. I sell children's (specifically baby and toddler) clothing and am starting to branch out into accessories. I started Brittain Road when my daughter was about a year old. I was looking for a creative outlet that I could do in the moments when she was asleep or otherwise occupied; I wanted to do something that would put me back in touch with a bigger group of people than I had access to as a stay-at-home mom. I actually first heard of Etsy on TV, during a morning talk show, and figured it might be just the right venue for the clothing I had recently started designing. It was very easy to sign up and get my store set up—and the rest is history.

Brittainroad.etsy.com

I studied Fine Arts in college and then got my degree in Interior Design. When I stopped working as a designer and decided to stay home with my daughter, I really missed working in a creative field. Also, when she was born, we were living in western Massachusetts, and it was a bit difficult to meet other women or moms that I felt I had a lot in common with. So, when I learned about Etsy and all the community there, it put me in touch with a lot of other creative people. I've never collaborated on a project there with anyone else, but I've spent lots of time discussing business and other aspects of running an Etsy shop with other sellers.

The type of clothing I design came about when I was overwhelmed by the frilly clothes that are often found for baby girls. I wanted to see things that were bright, funky, and certainly non-mainstream. I do make money from Etsy. Not a lot, and certainly not enough to support a family on. But I make enough to let me try out new ideas and cover my time. People seem to have found me mostly through Etsy searches or word of mouth. I've been lucky enough to be on a few blogs, including CoolMomPicks.com, which is pretty well-known.

I'd suggest anyone wanting to sell on Etsy have confidence in yourself and your product. Take excellent photos, and give outstanding customer service. Be sure to price your products well. Often I think people sell their handmade products for too little, and customers may get an inaccurate feel for how much time and energy was put into a really high-quality item.

WRITING

Freelance writers have found a new market online. Someone has to produce all that content, and that someone could be you! While you can do this occasionally as a source of side income, dedicated writers who spend more time writing and searching out higher-paying markets are able to create an entire freelance career out of their writing activities.

One option here is to write articles for sites that pay based either on the number of people who read your articles or the number of people who click on the ads placed on your article's site. These sites include:

- Associated Content (www.associatedcontent.com): Sign up to become a contributor on Associated Content, then receive a small flat fee plus additional payment based on how many page views your articles, videos, or photos receive. The site prefers "SEO-optimized" content, or articles that do well on keyword searches in the major search engines.

- eHow (ehow.com): Write "how-to" articles, and get paid based on the number of visitors your articles receive. Receive monthly PayPal payments any month your earnings top $10.

- Examiner.com (www.examiner.com/about_examiner): Check out Examiner.com, which looks for people to write local "insider" articles; writers are compensated based on a combination of page views, visitors, session length, and advertising performance. Payment is made through PayPal.

- Helium (www.helium.com): Find subjects looking for articles, write those articles, and get paid.

About.com offers a somewhat different model. Its "guides" to various topics are compensated in base pay plus increased compensation for growing

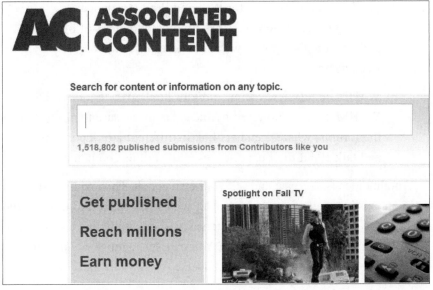

Associated Content

the page views on its site. Check available topics and find out more at beaguide.about.com/index.htm.

Beyond these sites, freelance writers have found that the internet opens up new opportunities, markets, and options. Some sites that often contain ads for freelance writing gigs include:

- craigslist (www.craigslist.org): Check your local craigslist, then move on to lists in other areas (especially major cities, since these locations receive more ads), because these are usually telecommuting gigs. Look in the "jobs" section under "writing/editing."

- Freelance Writing (www.freelancewriting.com/freelance-writing-jobs.php): Check out both help-wanted ads and gigs you can "bid" on.

- Freelance Writing Jobs for Web and Print (freelance writinggigs.com/webandprint): Find daily listings of blogging and writing gigs, plus a wealth of other information for freelancers.

- WAHM.com (www.wahm.com/jobs.html): While job ads at WAHM.com are powered by Indeed.com, be sure to also check the forums, where members link to different job opportunities and talk about their experiences with various companies.

Another idea is to create and sell your own ebook. This works best if you have an existing way of reaching people, such as a popular blog. If you run a blog with eBay selling tips, for instance, you might publish a companion ebook with bonus or advanced tips. You can self-publish ebooks at sites such as Lulu (www.lulu.com) and iUniverse (www.iuniverse.com).

BLOGGING

A spinoff of writing for other sites is blogging—for yourself or for others. (You can use some of the resources in this section if you run *any* kind of a website, blog or not.) There have been a number of articles lately on the recent phenomenon of "mommy bloggers," or blogging moms who focus on topics from family to frugality, with a personal twist. While the most famous might make "real" money at this, most people blog simply for the sake of blogging, and the bit of money they bring in becomes a bonus.

Learn from them and don't blog with the specific intention of making money. Blog because you have something to say to the world or because you have a passion for your subject. People will easily be able to tell if you blog simply for what little money there is to be had and will abandon your blog for others who blog because they *want* to—and with no readers, you have no revenue in any case. If you do choose to investigate the different ways of making money by blogging, though, take the time to build up your blog, your reputation, and your traffic first. Once you have a solid site and readership, you can look into several different options.

Another option is to blog for pay on other sites. Check out blogging job boards such as the one at ProBlogger (jobs.problogger.net) or sign up to blog for one of the more than 90 blogs at Weblogs, Inc. (www.weblogs inc.com). You'll do best if you already have a proven track record on your own or another blog. Be sure also to read the "Blogging for a Living" section at the Freelance Writing Jobs Network (freelancewritinggigs.com/ networkblogging).

You might also set up a blog to promote another business, or you could promote your business on an existing blog. If you have an Etsy store, for instance, talk about it and link to it on your blog. These things can feed into each other.

Launching a Blog

You can set up a blog very inexpensively—and in some cases for free! The free, and easiest, option is to use a site such as WordPress.com (wordpress.com). WordPress.com will host your site for you and provide you with free blogging tools to use. Want to become a better blogger? Check out BlogCoach (www.blogcoach.org), which is full of tips and tricks for bloggers new and old.

Affiliate Programs

An affiliate program lets you sign up to host ads on your site from various companies. You then generally get paid per click, per purchase, per ad view, or per some other action taken through these links. Most affiliate programs require that your blog—or any other website—already have fairly good traffic (monthly number of visitors) before they will let you join. Your internet service provider should be able to provide you with a way to retrieve these numbers; several third-party plug-ins for the various types of blogging software are also available to help you track your visitors. (For instance, you can get the stats plug-in for the popular WordPress application at wordpress.org/extend/plugins/stats.)

Be selective about the affiliate offers you post on your site. Add only those that are pertinent and don't go crazy. Again, readers will easily be able to tell if your blog becomes just an excuse to link to affiliates. Popular affiliate programs include:

- Amazon.com Associates (affiliate-program.amazon.com/gp/ associates/join): Amazon.com's affiliate program gives program participants a sliding percentage of each Amazon.com sale made through a link on the affiliate site. Affiliates can choose to receive payment via check, direct deposit, or Amazon.com gift certificates.

- Brandcaster (www.couponsinc.com/corp/brandcaster/home.html): Best for bargain or couponing blogs, the popular Coupons.com lets users print out manufacturer coupons for use in the store. When people click through and print Coupons.com coupons from your site, you, as a Brandcaster affiliate, will get a few cents per print.

- Commission Junction (www.cj.com): One of the largest and best-known affiliate programs, Commission Junction works with hundreds of advertisers. After you join Commission Junction, you'll have to apply individually through the Commission Junction site to become an affiliate for individual advertisers.

- Google Affiliate Network (www.google.com/ads/affiliatenetwork/ publisher/index.html): Google's program lets you connect with a number of large advertisers and works similarly to Commission Junction. This site doesn't work well in Firefox, so use Internet Explorer.

- LinkShare (www.linkshare.com): LinkShare is another very large affiliate network that lets you run ads from hundreds of different advertisers; it works similarly to Commission Junction.

- Logical Media (www.logicalmedia.com): Logical Media hosts a number of affiliate opportunities of varying legitimacy, so be choosy about those you include on your own blog. Advertisers pay per click, per sign-up, or per purchase, and the terms will be made clear when you choose to link to an offer.

- MySavings (partners.mysavings.com): MySavings is smaller than Logical Media but provides similar (and sometimes overlapping) affiliate opportunities.

- RedPlum (www.redplum.com): Another coupon printing site, RedPlum offers affiliates a few cents for each coupon printed through links back to RedPlum from the affiliate site.

Be aware that these programs do need to collect personal information (such as your Social Security number and a completed W9 form) in order to disburse payments. To avoid any concerns about sharing that kind of information, stick with large and well-known sites such as those listed here. On some, you'll need to register on the affiliate site and then be approved through that site by individual advertisers before running their ads.

Jaycie, a mom of two who blogs at Coupon Geek (www.coupongeek. net), says, "I blog mostly for fun and the joy of helping others. The money is just a bonus. If I focus too much on it, then it *really* feels like a job. Basically, I find the deals for my readers, and sometimes I post an ad or hook up with a new affiliate for sales commissions to let them help pay back some of what I have saved them. It all works out. I never post anything I don't think is a good deal, and I am very careful which companies I affiliate with. I've passed up on several money-makers because they didn't quite feel like they had my readers' best interests at heart." Readers quickly catch on to bloggers who blog for the affiliate income and not for their readers, so it's best to regard affiliate income as a nice bonus rather than a reason to blog.

ADVERTISING

Again, you're not likely to make a lot from advertising, especially at first, when you haven't yet built up a lot of traffic. The easiest way to place ads on your site is to sign up for Google's AdSense program (www.google. com/adsense). AdSense places contextual ads on sites. If you blog about a local store, for example, you might see an ad for that store pop up in the Google ads on your site. You then get paid by Google every time someone clicks on one of these ads (and that pay depends heavily on what kind of traffic your blog gets.) Google offers unobtrusive text link ads, so this is a good way to ease into advertising. Google issues checks monthly, but only when your AdSense account reaches $100 or more. You also have the option of embedding ads in the RSS feed for your blog in order to reach subscribers who read through a newsreader without visiting your actual site; FeedBurner (www.feedburner.com) will also let you embed your Google AdSense ads into your feeds.

If your blog reaches a primarily female audience, you can also look into the BlogHer ad network (www.blogherads.com). This one is open only occasionally, but you can sign up for its waiting list. It has a number of requirements for its blogging network, so be sure to read them before completing the sign up. One nice thing about BlogHer is that it pays per ad view rather than per person who clicks through.

REVIEWS

Some high-traffic bloggers are paid or otherwise compensated (usually in free products) to review items on their blogs. Be aware that you're walking a line: If you promote products you neither like nor use, simply because you got them for free, this is really an abuse of the trust your readers place in you to be unbiased and to work in their best interest. Give positive reviews only to products you truly feel positive about.

Some of these programs provide both products for you to review and giveaways for your readers. Two examples are MyBlogSpark (www.my blogspark.com) from General Mills and Mom Central Consulting (www.momcentralconsulting.com/index.php/join.html). Sign up with these sites to receive occasional emails about new programs you can participate in.

Then there's the option of writing sponsored content for various companies. Personally, this is where I feel bloggers tend to cross the line, but let me tell you what these posts involve so that you can decide for yourself. PayPerPost (www.payperpost.com), for instance, is the major site that compensates bloggers for writing sponsored content. Basically, it pays bloggers to review products, websites, companies, and services. There's an ethical line here that you want to be careful not to cross. Don't create a positive review for PayPerPost just for the money. Other sites that use a similar model are ReviewMe (www.reviewme.com), Blogsvertise (www.blogs vertise.com), and SponsoredReviews (www.sponsoredreviews.com). Be aware that if you write sponsored posts, you are disqualified from some popular ad networks, and you may alienate some of your readers.

ASKING FOR DONATIONS

If you are providing a service through your blog or website, you can ask your readers for donations. Just know going in that most people *won't* donate, because of the perception that everything is "free" on the internet. Some of your loyal users, though, might appreciate a way to give back. There are a couple of easy ways to place a donation option on your blog or site. If you use PayPal, for instance, you can place a PayPal *donation button* right on your website. PayPal will walk you step-by-step through creating the code to place on your blog (www.paypal.com/cgi-bin/webscr?cmd=_donate-intro-outside). Visitors can then click that button to easily make donations through PayPal. If you use WordPress for your blog, you can add the "Buy Me a Beer" WordPress plug-in (www.blogclout.com/blog/goodies/buy-me-a-beer-paypal-donation-plugin).

MYSTERY SHOPPING

Talk about a perfect gig: getting paid to shop! Before getting started as a mystery (or secret) shopper, make sure that you're signing up with a reputable company. You can check the Mystery Shopping Providers Association (MSPA; www.mysteryshop.org/shoppers/membercos.php) to see whether the company you're thinking of working with is certified, and you can check the forums on Volition.com (forum.volition.com/forum.asp?FORUM_ID=3) to read about others' experiences with different companies.

Mystery shopping can take a while to break into. You'll need to take lower-paying opportunities at first while you're building up your reputation, and you can also get certified as a mystery shopper yourself at the MSPA. Make sure you're detail-oriented, because you will need to write up detailed reports on the shops that you cover. Realize also that you generally pay up front for the items or services you buy when doing a mystery shop, and it takes some time to get reimbursed. Never, ever pay the company you're working with a fee to get started, though!

Some mystery shopping sites to start with include IntelliShop (www.intelli-shop.com), Volition.com (www.volition.com/mystery.html), and JobSlinger (www.jobslinger.com). At each of these, find out more about mystery shopping and sign up for possible gigs.

Alli D. is a couponer and mother of two.

I started doing mystery shopping during grad school as a way to keep myself busy and earn a bit of extra money. I have always had a strange knack for finding ways to make or save money. My husband thinks this is hilarious and just smiles when I tell him about the new thing I've found.

There are honestly too many mystery shopping companies to list, as I think I'm signed up with close to 70 (although some have probably closed now). The best way that I have found to weed the legitimate ones out from the others is through Volition.com, which has an area specifically for mystery shopping (www.volition.com/mystery.html). Companies are listed A to Z (and it takes a lot of time to get through them all, let me tell you!), and a bit is written about each company. Before joining, I then cross-reference the company with the forum information (forum.volition.com/forum.asp?FORUM_ID=3) to make sure that no one is having problems with payment, etc.

I get emailed at least 50 opportunities a day, but most are not convenient for me, not worth the money for the drive required, out of state, or not a job I enjoy doing. But I am picky these days because I can be. If you wanted to take anything you could get, you would probably have lots of opportunities. Everything is done online before and after the visit. You receive your instructions and information online and then visit the store during your assigned time. You perform your shop (these are usually very natural shopping experiences), submit your report online, take a picture to upload your receipt and business card, and get paid at the end of the following month.

I can't be specific about actual mystery shops I've done, because you agree to that upon signing up, but generally (and feel free to use your imagination!), I have visited coffeehouses, office supply stores, restaurants, banks, retail stores, grocery stores, [and] oil change locations, made phone calls, and [done] lots more that I can't think of. There are also opportunities available at hotels, airports, car dealerships, apartment rental companies, healthcare companies, and probably anything else you can imagine.

Depending on the shop, you will typically make between $7 and $10 for a basic retail shop (plus reimbursement for the purchase you are required to make) and more for the more involved shops (if you have to test drive a car, etc.). I enjoy the flexibility, the fact that I don't have to take any shops I don't want to, that I can bring my children on most shops, and that I can get paid for doing something I was going to do anyway.

If you're just getting started in mystery shopping, start with Volition.com! And do not under any circumstances respond to an email telling you that you can make $400 per month by sending them your information, your local Walmart address, and your local currency exchange address! Remember, a job will typically only pay around $8. I believe the most I've ever been paid was $50, and that is almost unheard of now.

DIRECT SALES

You've heard of Tupperware. But have you heard of Tastefully Simple, Pampered Chef, PartyLite, Usborne Books, and Silpada jewelry? All of these companies sign up women to make direct sales through *home parties*, selling items to their friends, relatives, and neighbors at these events and keeping a commission on each item sold. Plus, most of these organizations also offer special hostess discounts and prizes based on sales. If you have a large circle of friends and family to get you started, and if you have an outgoing personality and love to host get-togethers, you might think about joining one of these programs. (And you can serve some of those cheap-after-coupon treats to your guests!) Direct sales can be a great field when you're working around kids' schedules, since these parties generally take place in the evenings and on the weekends.

Most direct sales consultants earn just a couple of hundred dollars a month, although this is another field where you earn back just as much as you put into it. If you want to earn just a bit on the side, then it can be a fun part-time activity. If you want to turn it into a more serious part-time job, then you'll need to put more effort into hosting parties and recruiting others. Think about your goals before you jump in.

If you're considering direct sales, be sure to research the company before signing up. Ask yourself questions like: What am I getting into? What rules will I have to follow? What kind of initial investment do I have to make? Is this a known brand name? Would I buy these products myself? Will my friends and family be interested in these types of products? Am I comfortable with the thought of going out and finding new customers after I have tapped into my existing friends and family network? Am I outgoing enough to run these parties? What are my goals—to turn this into a part-time job, or to just make a little money on the side?

Also keep in mind that direct sales can be the one exception to never putting out an initial investment for a work-at-home job, because some of these jobs require you to invest in products to sell up-front. So factor the start-up costs into your decision. You should be able to find out these costs from the company, and they shouldn't be more than a couple hundred dollars. Also ask the company what kind of training program it offers new consultants to help you get started.

You'll do best if you choose a direct sales company that you love and whose products you use. You can't "sell" products that you're not interested in. So attend a party or two yourself, try out the products, and spend some quality time on the company's website perusing the products. And be sure you're self-motivated because no one will be standing over you requiring you to put in the time. Find out more about direct sales at the Direct Selling Association (www.dsa.org).

In Her Own Words

Victoria H. is an independent Tastefully Simple consultant (www.tastefullysimple.com) and mother of three.

When my second son was 4 months old, I overheard a girl at my La Leche League meeting talking to the group leader about how she did taste-testing parties with a company called Tastefully Simple. I got the info from her, and then I hosted a taste-testing party. I was impressed by how delicious the products were and how they made me feel like I could be a better cook by using them. Considering that everyone eats, I figured maybe I could do what this girl did!

I had one goal in mind at the time: I needed a job that would allow me to make up the $150 a week I had lost when my second son was born. At that point, I couldn't continue with my 2-day-a-week job, because no family members wanted to watch my almost-2-year-old and 4-month-old for free. When you only make

$150 a week, what would be left after day care? So I talked with the consultant, found that a goal of $150 weekly profit was reasonable, and joined Tastefully Simple. That was 7 years ago.

Tastefully Simple is a direct sales company. Basically, as consultants, we set our own hours, grow our own clientele, and are paid on commission. We are known for our home taste-testing parties, where a host invites her friends over, everyone tastes samples of our food products, and people can choose to place orders for everything they enjoyed. These include spices, sauces, [and] marinades. We help people make restaurant-quality food at home and provide shortcuts to great food!

What I like most about being a consultant with Tastefully Simple is all the great people I have connected with. I have a great job because I'm always going to a different office, I am not looking at the same cubicle, and I'm not dealing with office politics. The icing on the cake is that I control my own schedule and earnings.

For some people, Tastefully Simple is a way to earn an extra income on the side. For me, it has always been my part-time job. At this point, because I earn monthly bonuses for leading a team of other consultants, I am earning quite a bit more than I would at a traditional part-time job. I ask my party hosts if they'd like to learn more about what I do, because one of the reasons people host taste-testings is they are interested in getting a feel for what I do. Party hosts also tend to have a love for our products. Also, some people ask me about the business, the most popular question being: Do you really make money doing this? So we talk about it. If they decide they'd like to join, then I become their "sponsor," which means I train them and cheer them on. I enjoy being a leader, because I like what I do and I like sharing the opportunity with others. I partner with people—I'm not a "boss." If you're interested in getting started in direct sales:

1. Take your calendar and mark off all your personal obligations and family time, then circle the days you want to schedule parties or business exposure events.

2. Share with everyone that you have started a home-based business. You may be surprised who turns out to be your first clients.

3. When choosing a direct sales company, go with a company whose products you believe in and love. Share your passion with others!

When I began with Tastefully Simple, I had two boys under 2, and a couple years later I had a baby girl. Using the internet has been the key to my business. I can contact people, place orders, and follow up with clients and team members early in the morning or at night. Email allows me to "speak" to clients without having to worry about kids running around, the dog barking, etc. I market my Tastefully Simple business online in several ways:

- I use email to contact and follow up with clients.

- I have a blog that I use to share details about my life and recipes.

- I use Facebook to connect with clients and friends.

- I have a company-provided webpage that people can order through or contact me from.

- I email a newsletter to clients and team members.

I especially enjoy connecting through Facebook, because it allows me to connect with my clients as well as other consultants. It's fun to be able to wish one of my hosts a happy birthday or see that a team member has had a business success. Facebook also allows me to share with my clients, colleagues, and friends the good things in my life and my business successes—and this leads to new business and new connections for me. Facebook helps me to further my belief about running a successful business: When you value the relationships your business allows you to create, a successful business will follow.

I also belong to a Yahoo! Group with members of other direct sales companies. I network with other Tastefully Simple consultants through a company-provided message board forum, through Facebook, and through MyFamily pages (myfamily.com)—which we use as a message board. And I occasionally use an online survey creator to survey my clients' needs and wants. By using an online point-and-click survey, I get a much larger response than in the past, when I did paper surveys through the mail, and what I have found is pretty interesting. In the past (prior to the economic downturn), when asked what type of "sales" or specials they would like to see offered, the majority said percent-off sales. This year, when asked, the majority said they'd prefer a gift with purchase.

The biggest benefit for me of being a Tastefully Simple independent consultant is that I am now more than ever using our products to make meals at home instead of succumbing to the siren call of the drive-through or carry out. Anyone with a family knows that food costs have been taking a larger and larger part of a household budget. Because our products are concentrated, I can use our sauces with cheaper cuts of meat. I also use some of our spices in a variety of ways in a recipe so that I don't have to buy several products (for example, I use Garlic Garlic for fresh garlic, minced garlic, garlic salt, and garlic powder). This gives me more money [for] stocking up on good deals with my coupons on name-brand products like shampoo, chocolate, etc. I also take advantage of store savings cards (such as Staples Rewards) to reap extra rewards on business supplies I'd need to buy anyway.

The economy has affected my business in a few ways. First, it has given me the opportunity to share with clients how to use our products to stretch their grocery dollars. In the past they may have been more likely to purchase our desserts; now they are more likely to purchase spices and sauces that can be used many times over. Second, I hear about so many people who've lost their jobs or had their hours cut. Because of this, I have had more people asking me to share how Tastefully Simple works—they're looking for a new way to bring back some of the income they have lost.

Nonprofit and community groups have also been contacting me for information on fundraising or asking that I make a donation of gift baskets. Many report that they are scrambling to raise funds because the larger companies and corporations that have supported them in the past are now unable to donate. And I am happy to help. One of the nice things about my Tastefully Simple business is that, through my business, I am able to support more great causes and groups than I would ever be able to do through my personal household budget.

TAKE YOUR SAVINGS SKILLS ON THE ROAD

Once you've become an expert at saving for your own family, why not put those skills to work in helping others who are more pressed for time or who don't know quite where to begin? Everyone can use some help finding ways to save in this economy, so think about ways to market your new-found skills and knowledge to others.

COUPON CLASSES

You've become a coupon queen! Or at least figured you've out the basic strategies that allow you to save substantially on groceries and everyday household goods each week. Why not teach others to do the same thing? Sometimes, people just appreciate the hands-on opportunity, and some learn better by actually seeing how these strategies work.

Conducting coupon classes can be one of the most natural ways to mash up a money-saving, money-making life. Share the secrets you've learned with others, and get paid for doing so! If you think you might be interested in doing something like this, start by talking to your local library; they're always looking for people to offer new programs and classes, and this is the perfect time to start. Read the earlier sections on starting your own blog if you're thinking of teaching—these activities can feed into one another.

In Her Own Words

Jill Cataldo teaches Super-Couponing work-shops, writes the syndicated "The Coupon Queen" column, and blogs at jillcataldo.com.

I started teaching Super-Couponing in August 2008. In March of that year, our local library was looking for new program ideas, and I approached it about teaching a class. We live in a small town, and [the library] said that if the class attracted 20 to 30 people, we'd have a resounding success; 162 people registered, and I very quickly found myself with a new job! In my Super-Couponing workshops, I teach couponing basics—different types of coupons, why it's important to save all our coupons (even ones for items we don't think we want), and how to organize them in a fast, easy system that can be done in a half hour to an hour each week. The techniques I teach will easily cut anyone's grocery bill 30 to 50 percent and often even more.

I'm seeing huge turnouts: If the venues have the capacity, I typically teach to over 100 people a night. With three to four classes a week, I'm teaching a very large number of people on a weekly basis. Clearly, the economy has driven much of this, but there's a definite fun factor in this too. Getting great deals on items your household needs and wants anyway often brings a thrill—and the sometimes mundane task of shopping can become an adventure. And when people hear that they could be saving over half their grocery bill each week, they're interested!

This is actually a great time to get started saving. While the economy is bad, it's a great time to be a shopper. We're seeing things go on sale and clearance prices more frequently, with deeper discounts than ever before—and one of the methods I teach is to stock up on whatever it is, before you need it, buying it at the time when the store's getting rid of it. Don't buy a new lawnmower in the spring—buy it in the fall, when the snow blowers are hitting the stores. Buy children's summer clothes at the end of *this* summer, when they're reduced beyond belief. These things have just become second nature to me.

With the continued success of the classes, I was approached in October 2008 about writing a syndicated newspaper column on coupons. "The Coupon Queen" was born, and as of this writing, it's syndicated in over a hundred markets nationally to a weekly readership of over 11 million. The column has been extremely fun for me, too, as I'm a writer at heart—I have a strong journalism background and worked in print media for a long time prior to becoming a Coupon Queen. And, it's a fantastic job for a mom to have; I can write my columns on my laptop while playing with my kids at home.

Learn to Super-Coupon®!

Submitted by Coupon Maven on Wed, 01/20/2010 - 11:18

Do you feel like you're spending too much money on groceries? Want to learn a fun, easy way to save money and shop smarter?

With Super-Couponing®, you'll learn how to maximize your grocery savings and purchase hundreds of dollars worth of groceries for pennies! I'll teach you the couponing secrets of the pros, which stores will let you stack multiple coupons, how to track sales and discounts online, and best of all - how to get the store to pay you to shop.

You'll also learn the number one mistake most couponers make, as well as an efficient way to plan your shopping trips in the least amount of time for the most effective savings.

The following Super-Couponing® and Super-Couponing® 2 classes are scheduled for the Chicagoland area. Call or visit the website of the class provider to register. All classes held at public libraries are FREE!

Early registration is recommended as these workshops tend to fill up quickly! Unless otherwise noted, all library workshops are free to attend. Additionally, it is <u>highly</u> recommended that you attend Super-Couponing® before attending Super-Couponing® 2 as a large portion of the second class builds on principles taught in the first.

Jill Cataldo's Super-Couponing classes

With the success of the newspaper column, I started receiving numerous requests from my readers in markets around the nation wishing to attend the class—but logistically, I do teach the majority of my classes close to home, near Chicago. So I began thinking about recording my live class for a DVD release. Video production is expensive, but this felt like a risk worth taking because my column reader base is so strong that I thought I'd eventually break even, at the very least. And, as altruistic as it sounds, I genuinely wanted to get this material out there and available to everyone who wished to learn. I have seen firsthand what a difference something as seemingly simple as cutting the grocery bill can do for households and families. When the DVD came out and the first emails and blog posts from people who had purchased it started coming in, I knew we had a winner—the class translated very well to video and has the benefit of re-watchability, too.

Believe it or not, I do very little marketing for the classes. They sell themselves. I primarily try to speak at libraries, because while libraries budget a stipend for their guest speakers, they typically do not pass this fee along to their patrons. This was always a big part of my local business model—people shouldn't have to pay much, if anything, to learn how to SAVE money! And word spreads quickly when something is good, free, and popular— word of mouth keeps my classes full and my schedule busy. With the exception of my first class, I've never actively sought another booking for a workshop: They all come to me based on what they're hearing from attendees and other venues that have previously hosted classes. That's a nice position to be in, as my schedule is typically booked solid 6 to 9 months ahead.

I do also have a recurring radio segment on coupons on the largest rock radio station in Chicago, and that's been phenomenal to help keep my name out there and draw interest for my classes. One of the biggest misconceptions people have is that couponing is a "women's thing." If a *coupon* segment can fly on a male-oriented rock station for over 9 months straight, you know there are men interested in this topic, too. On any given day, typically 20 to 30 percent of my audience is made up of men, and they're very, very good at couponing.

I have two sites: My SuperCouponing.com site is devoted to my classes directly, and you'll find video clips, my speaking schedule, and some of the coupon tools I discuss in class there. My blog, jillcataldo.com, has really grown into an animal, though. I started blogging in July 2008, after I had responded to a callout in the *Chicago Sun-Times* for readers to tell the editors how they were saving on groceries. The response to that initial article was phenomenal, and numerous people suggested I start blogging.

With the blog, I have always tried to create the kind of site I *wished* existed when I was learning to do this. When you are first starting out, it helps to have someone tell you exactly what you need to do to break down a sale—buy this, this, and this, use these coupons, and it will cost you this. There are plenty of blogs doing "best-deals" or coupon matchups, but I focus on a few simple, high-value deals each week from a variety of stores local to Chicago. And once someone gets a taste of their first 6-cent jar of applesauce, or better yet, matches a $1 coupon to a $1 sale and takes that item home for free, they're on their way to learning how to spot those deals themselves.

I have always used coupons—always. But I wasn't using them like this until around 3 years ago, when we were pregnant with our third child. As a stay-at-home mom, I realized when the new baby came, we'd have two in diapers instead of one, and I thought it was time to really start watching and saving on at least that one item—diapers! I'd occasionally see stories on the news about other coupon queens buying hundreds of dollars worth of items for pennies, and I thought, I want to *be* one of those people. So I started really digging into and researching the best ways people use coupons to get those high-value discounts.

Couponing has also allowed me to give an incredible amount of food and supplies to our local food pantry. That's one thing people who've never couponed find hard to believe—we do get a lot of things for free with coupons, typically many more than one household can reasonably use. I am at our local food pantry almost every week dropping off groceries and helping out, often with my children in tow! But I think that's an important thing for them to see, too. While we're doing fine, many people are struggling right now, and anything I buy that we will not use or need goes straight to the pantry—typically six to eight bags worth of groceries at a time.

It's funny—while I've always been a money saver who enjoyed getting the best prices on everything I buy, I never intended to go into business for myself. But now that I'm here, I have found it to be a wonderful mix of both worlds. I'm saving money *and* earning it by sharing what I've learned with others.

PERSONAL SHOPPING

Since you're now an expert shopper—right?—another way to put those skills to good use is by helping others who are too busy to learn the ropes or do the deals. Some couponers jump into being personal shoppers for family or friends, taking a commission or regular payment for finding them the best deals and doing their shopping for them.

It can take some time to get into personal shopping and to find the right clients to shop for. But as long as you're doing the deals for yourself, why not also think about doing them for others!

In Her Own Words

Sati of CafeMom is a personal shopper.

I work as a personal assistant and personal shopper to a woman who has two full-time jobs. She loves to work but works so much she cannot manage mundane things. I do those things for her *plus* save her money. She spends less paying me to shop for her than she would shopping on her own. I do most of her shopping, with the exception of clothes shopping, although I often try to find sales or coupons for the stores she likes. She works four jobs throughout the year, two full-time and two part-time, so between it all she really has *no* time to really learn to *save* money.

I have known her for 12 years. Over time, she started asking me to pick up this or that if it was on sale, and she would pay me back. Eventually I just offered to do *all* her grocery and personal shopping for her. I know her general likes and dislikes, and when I see something she likes on sale, I get it. She might not need it right at that moment, but I know she will, so I stockpile it until she wants it.

I have not yet decided if I am expanding to personal shopping for other people. It's not very easy to keep track of, so while it works for me and her, I am not sure about someone that I don't know so well. My suggestion to someone who wants to do this is do it for someone they know *well* first, before expanding.

Use Your Existing Skills

A lot of stay-at-home or suddenly-out-of-work moms (and dads) use their existing skills to create a new business. Teachers turn to tutoring, moms start a home day care, musicians offer private music lessons, designers sell WordPress templates or web design services. In any of these cases, you can use online resources to advertise your business and to network with others—and in some cases can turn your skills into an entirely online job.

Think about what else you can do, or what you'd like to do. Do you love kids? Are you artistic? Do you know how to write computer programs, were you a graphic designer in a former life, are you crafty, can you sell anything to anyone? Start by writing down all your skills and hobbies, even if they don't seem "marketable" on the face of things. You'll probably be surprised by the patterns you see emerging. Ask family and friends what *they* think you're best at—it's always useful to get an outside perspective.

Tracy F., a mother of three, is a home day care provider and Usborne books consultant.

I am a home day care provider. I chose this type of "work" to do from home because I really wanted to be able to stay home with my children. I was previously a teacher, and I love children, so really don't consider what I do work. This is the best of both worlds! I do get to bring in some money for our family, while still having my dream of staying home with my kids. I feel having other kids at our home is also beneficial for my children. It helps with socialization and teaches them how to share and take turns, plus they love having "friends" over to play. I have the best "job" in the world!

The internet is my main source for posting my openings when looking for children to care for. I mainly use craigslist to post my ads but have used other online sites. I am part of a few mom groups that have message boards, so am able to ask there if they know of anyone who is in need of child care. Email is usually the first line of communication when speaking with a potential client. Word-of-mouth has also helped me find children to care for, but online resources are the main way I have been able to continue to care for children out of my home. I also use the internet to find activities for the kids to do [and] new places to take them and to talk with other day care providers to see what's working for them and to set up playdates.

Our family has also recently started selling things on eBay and craigslist to try to generate a little extra income, and I have just started selling children's books through Usborne Books. As a teacher, I feel that books are valuable tools that every home should have. This is a way for me to continue "teaching" while helping families connect with their children, and it also helps bring in a little more money for our family.

If I were not able to do home day care, I would certainly need to work outside the home. The extra money we make from home day care, selling things online, selling children's books, and saving money all around enable me to stay home. If we didn't use coupons, didn't bring in any "extra" income, and didn't try to save money, we would not be able to afford to have a "stay-at-home mom."

Because of the current economic situation, we certainly do not go out to eat as much, and we have started a budget for our eating-out expenses. In the past, we would eat out when we wanted and not really consider where it would be "cheapest" to eat. We now use coupons whenever we do go out to eat, and we try to find restaurants where children eat for free to save money.

The economy has affected our shopping/saving habits as well. Now we always think about what we are purchasing (do we really need this?). I was never a "coupon clipper," but now I go through the paper and search online for coupons before we go anywhere. I also subscribe to a wonderful blog where coupons and money-saving strategies are given to me. Now, I go to different stores to see their prices and use the internet to find the best price on things before we buy them; I use PriceGrabber.com to find the best price of any given item.

If you're interested in doing home day care, research it before you start. Find out what you need to make in order to stay home. You may think you can watch one child and that will be enough, but that's not necessarily the case. Are you the type of person who can "handle" having lots of kids around? I know someone who started a home day care with the intention of watching one child. That was not enough income for her family, so then she needed to take on a few more children. She came to despise watching kids and went back to working full-time.

Find out how much other providers (both home and centers) in the area are charging. Talk to others who do home day care to find out how they "do it" and what's really involved. Talk to people you know to see if anyone they know is in need of child care. When and if you post online, give details—what types of activities you do, how your day will run, your experience with children, etc.

Be patient. Don't just "take" the first child that comes along. You need to make sure the child/family is a good fit with you and your family. You will develop a relationship with this family, so you all need to be on the same page. You need to make sure, if you have children, that they all get along—not all kids do.

Most important, make sure you *want* to do this. Watching children is one of the most important jobs you will ever have. You are responsible for this child's health, safety, and overall well-being. It is important that you *love* what you do.

LOOK FOR GIGS

There are a number of sites that list freelance and work-at-home gigs. These include:

- craigslist (www.craigslist.com): Check the appropriate craigslist categories in your local area, and then look in other large urban areas. People often post freelance and telecommuting gigs only on their own craigslist, even though these are open to anyone, anywhere.

- Elance (www.elance.com): Companies post jobs they need done on Elance, and then you bid on these jobs by submitting a proposal. One problem with Elance and other "bid for gigs" sites is that so many people are competing for work that it tends to drive the rates down—so be aware of this going in.

- GetAFreelancer (www.getafreelancer.com): This one is for programmers, web designers, copy writers, and translators; as with Elance, you bid on posted projects.

- Guru (www.guru.com): Post your profile on Guru, which is very similar to Elance, and then search for and submit quotes for the projects that clients list.

- Inc. Moms (incmoms.com/category/work-at-home/work-at-home-jobs): This site pulls telecommuting ads from Indeed.com, which Indeed.com gets from a number of job and freelance sites.

- LiveWork (www.livework.com): Sign up at LiveWork to search and apply for contract projects in a variety of areas.

- oDesk (www.odesk.com): Sign up here for email notifications of jobs that match your categories. The rates here, especially for freelance writing jobs, are exceptionally low—I just looked at several that paid around $1 to $2 per 500- to 1,000-word article.

- Skillance (www.skillance.com): Contractors search this site for people who possess given skills for projects they need to staff.

- WAHM.com (www.wahm.com/jobs.html): Find work-at-home job listings from Indeed.com. Also explore the WAHM.com

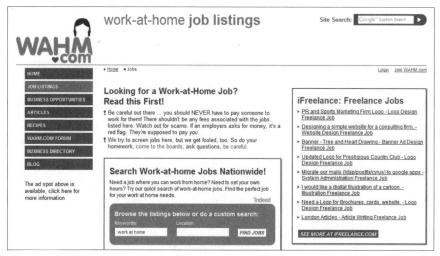

Job listings at WAHM.com

forums, where people talk about their experiences and share
further opportunities.

While the get-a-gig sites can be useful, they don't tend to result in a lot
of well-paying gigs. Most of your freelance work—especially at first—will
likely come via referrals from people who know you and what you have to
offer. Make sure that your whole network knows that you're now freelancing, because who knows who they know or what skills they might need?
This includes both people you know online and people you know in the real
world. It's OK and accepted to let your Facebook friends know what you're
up to.

Also look for niche sites to help you find freelance work in your area of
expertise. Here are just a few ideas:

- Photographers can search for gigs at Freelance Photo Jobs
  (www.freelancephotojobs.com).

- Computer programmers looking for contract work can try RentACoder (www.rentacoder.com).

- Teachers or others with an education background can sign up to provide homework help and tutoring online at Tutor.com (www.tutor.com/apply). Tutor.com looks for math, science, English, and social studies tutors, especially during the high-volume homework hours of late afternoon and evening Sundays through Thursdays. Or consider scoring essays and tests online for a company such as Pearson Education (www.pearsoned measurement.com and click "scoring at home"). Pearson also hires temporary scorers to score tests at its regional centers—the timing is based around the different exams, so it's possible to work this around your husband's vacation or other schedules. Scoring for Pearson requires just a bachelor's degree, although any other qualifications you have are sure to help.

- Do you have a pleasant phone voice, enjoy helping people, and want flexible hours? Sign up with Convergys (www.convergys. com), LiveOps (www.liveops.com), or Alpine Access (www. alpineaccess.com/en/apply) to take customer service, sales, or tech support calls from your home office around your kids' school schedules.

If you eventually find yourself wanting to work out of the house part-time, you might want to look for jobs at stores that give an employee discount (your local grocery store, home improvement store, clothing store—especially as fill-in Christmas help). Use sites such as Indeed (indeed.com) that aggregate job postings from a number of places to help you find part-time work.

USE ONLINE TOOLS

Why pay for expensive tools and software to help you run your home business or freelance, when you can find plenty of free tools online? Here are a few sites to check out:

- FreelanceSwitch.com rates calculator (freelanceswitch.com/rates): This interactive application helps you figure out what you should be charging for different services.

- Mashable.com (mashable.com/2008/09/21/270-online-business-tools): Mashable.com has a list of 270+ tools for running your business online, which also links to the previous year's tools. You'll definitely find something in here you can use!

- Zoho invoices (invoice.zoho.com/login/jsp/login.jsp): This site can help you create and manage professional-looking invoices online.

Also check CNET's download.com for other free and low-cost business software ideas.

SORT OUT THE SCAMS

If you've spent any time online, you know that the internet is full of scammers and spammers. Some unscrupulous individuals find it even easier to scam others online than in real life. Because these folks know that a lot of internet users are looking to make money online, some focus their scamming efforts on that area.

Some of these scams are fairly easy to spot: Something that promises thousands of dollars for just a few hours of work a week? Scam. Anything full of blinking pop-ups? Scam. Some, though, are less easy to figure out. Some resources that can be helpful in spotting scams include:

- Better Business Bureau (bbb.org): Find out whether anyone has filed a complaint against a given company.

- Federal Trade Commission (ftc.gov/bcp/menus/consumer/ education/jobs.shtm): Read information from the FTC about a number of popular scams.

- Google (www.google.com): On Google (yes, Google!), search for the name of the company you're thinking of signing up with, but add words such as *scam* or *fraud* or *complaint*. You just might find disgruntled folks talking about their experiences.

- Social networking sites: Connect with other work-at-home folks on Facebook (www.facebook.com) and LinkedIn (www.linkedin. com), and tap into that network with questions about companies you're considering working with.

- Work-at-home sites: Use the forums on sites like WAHM.com to ask about specific companies and read about others' experiences.

Overall, if something just seems too good to be true, it probably is. Also watch out for lots of exclamation points, misspellings, and other clues that the poster is not really a legitimate business. Rat Race Rebellion (www.ratracerebellion.com/spottingscams.html) has some useful info on spotting scams.

MASH IT UP

The possibilities here are nearly endless; you can mix and match multiple money-making opportunities in the right combination for you. How much extra time do you have? How much extra money do you need to bring in? You can sell on eBay *and* host Tastefully Simple parties *and* answer online surveys—whatever works for you. The more activities you combine, and the more streams of income you have, the more potential you have for bringing in money. Finding the right balance for you also includes finding the right balance of money-making activities. Some of these things you can also just dip into to see if they're right for you. Experiment with a blog or with Etsy or with selling on eBay. If you find it's not right, you can move on to something else.

We tend to put ourselves in a little box—I'm a stay-at-home mom, I'm a file clerk, I'm a librarian—when in reality, we can combine multiple money-making opportunities and enjoy the best of several worlds. Make a little here, a little there, and you'll probably be surprised by how it starts to add up—it's like the latte factor in reverse! One of my very favorite books, Barbara J. Winter's *Making a Living Without a Job*, talks about the idea of "multiple profit centers," or of bringing in income from multiple sources. When you find multiple ways to bring in income, you don't have to make as much from any one source; it's a lot easier to add up $250 a month doing this and $250 a month doing that than to make $500 a month on just one activity. Carly R., an Ohio mother of one who scores for Educational Testing Service and does online tutoring for Brainfuse, among other things, explains: "I guess I think that all of the different things that I do are a part-time job when considered together. I am always on the lookout for 'multiple streams of income,' so to speak, so that combined effort does seem to be a part time job. If I were only doing one thing, it would be more like just extra income."

When we use multiple strategies for bringing in income, we're also less dependent on one employer or one method. This is a plus in tough economic times; as we have all seen, even the seemingly most stable jobs or companies aren't necessarily so. If one company you work with goes under or cuts back, you'll still have your other streams of income to draw on. Read on to learn about other ways to mash up a bit more income with your work-at-home and savings strategies.

8

Make Bonus Income
With Your Online Activities

While you're spending all this time online anyway, why not devote a bit of that time to earning a little money from your online activities? Companies and marketers are always looking for feedback and insight into consumer behavior. They've realized that there's a critical mass of people right at their fingertips on the internet, and they now pay people to do everything online from watch ads to answer surveys, search, and click through on emails. Why not answer surveys from your laptop while watching TV at night or click through on a couple of ads while reading email each morning?

These sites pay out in varying ways: actual checks (or PayPal deposits), gift cards, or opportunities to earn points and then redeem them for merchandise in the site's online store. Other sites pay people in similar ways to answer questions or complete tasks online. Some of these gigs may sound similar to the work-from-home options in Chapter 7, but most of the opportunities I'm talking about here will only provide bonus income rather than full-time-job-replacing income. But these activities don't tend to take much time and can easily fit into a busy schedule.

Mash up your bonus online income and your work-at-home income with all of your savings strategies to really see the benefits of these online resources. When you've reduced your grocery bill by 50 percent or more, somehow the small bonus income you earn on these sites doesn't seem so small after all—you can buy a lot of cheap groceries and toiletries with the bits of money you make!

GET PAID TO TAKE SURVEYS

There are a number of survey sites online, some more trustworthy than others. One basic rule of thumb is to avoid participating in anything that requires you to complete "offers" (that is, to put out your own money to purchase products or services) in order to be eligible. Along the same lines, never join a survey site that requires you to pay a fee to participate. You will, however, need to fill out profiles on these sites and answer surveys that sometimes ask for a good deal of personal information. This is because the companies who do market research through survey sites usually want to target a specific segment of the population. If you're ever uncomfortable answering any of the questions, simply close that particular survey and move on.

Many survey sites are specifically looking for moms to give their input—good news for us mashup moms! Here are just a few valid and popular sites:

- Daily Survey Panel (www.dailysurveypanel.com): This site offers a number of daily surveys and pays out via PayPal or gift cards. Its minimum payout threshold, unlike most survey sites, is a low $1, which is paid within a couple of days. The site also has a referral program: If a friend signs up under your link, you'll receive $1 per month for as long as that person remains an active member and continues taking surveys on the site.

- DollarSurveys.net (www.dollarsurveys.net): Take a survey, and get a dollar in your PayPal account. It's just that simple. This site does include "offers" in some of its surveys, so just skip right over any of those.

- Ipsos i-Say (www.i-say.com): Earn points for each completed survey and then redeem your points for gift cards and merchandise on the site. After each survey you complete, you also get a chance to play in sweepstakes for items such as laptops and TVs.

- MindField Online (www.mindfieldonline.com): This site has a lower payout threshold than some. You can cash out via check or PayPal once you hit $5 in your account.

- MySurvey.com (www.mysurvey.com): This pays the equivalent of 5 to 10 cents for each short "qualifying" survey—but then, when you "qualify," you get the opportunity to take a higher-paid survey and/or do a product test. (Most sites pay nothing at all if you fill out the initial survey and don't "qualify," so it's not as bad as it sounds.) You can also refer your friends and receive 150 "points" (the equivalent of $1.50) for each referral. Redeem points for cash or merchandise; you can cash out once you get more than 1,000 points (the equivalent of $10).

- Opinion Outpost (www.opinionoutpost.com): Take surveys to earn "opinion points." Each opinion point is worth 10 cents, and you can cash out at $5; payment is via check. To earn additional opinion points, you can refer friends.

- Surveyhead (www.surveyhead.com): You get a $5 sign-up bonus just for joining, so that's a plus, and payout is via PayPal. What's nice about Surveyhead is that it estimates the odds of your getting accepted into each survey and tells you up front how much each pays in cash, so no messing around with "points."

- Valued Opinions (www.valuedopinions.com): Valued Opinions deposits a reward (generally $1 to $5) into your account for each survey you complete, and you will have the occasional opportunity to do product tests. Once your account reaches $20, you can cash out for prizes such as Amazon.com gift certificates.

When you click on a survey opportunity through email or at any of these sites, most will require you first to complete some "screening" questions to see if you qualify. This can be frustrating because these qualifiers are sometimes quite lengthy; so you may spend your time answering a number of questions only to find out you don't qualify for the actual, paying survey. Over time, though, you'll get a feeling for which sites are the best fit and which are most likely to result in paying surveys for you.

MySurvey.com

Beyond paying you to complete surveys, many survey sites offer additional points or payment for each friend you refer to the service. This works out best if you have a blog or other online presence with which you can reach a large number of potential sign-ups at once; you can also refer friends who'd like to make a bit of money on the side themselves. Avoid "spamming" people—only email people you know and who are truly interested. Other sites, such as the popular PineCone Research (www.pinecone research.com), are open by invitation only. They accept a certain number of new members and then close their doors again until the next enrollment period.

When you sign up for survey sites, be sure to use your free email account or set up a new one for this purpose. When survey invitations appear in your email, click through and answer as soon as possible. These surveys tend to fill up fast and will close once they've reached a certain number of participants. Use a program such as RoboForm (www.robo form.com/download.html) to automatically fill out some of the standard information these surveys most commonly ask for.

No one gets rich on survey sites, but if you spend some time here, you can earn enough money or gift certificates to pay for Christmas or otherwise cover the "extras" that are often hard to afford in tough economic times. Not facing big credit card bills in January? Priceless. On sites that pay by check, try to deposit these checks into a separate account immediately upon receipt so that you never see that money in your main checking account and aren't tempted to spend it. Build up this account for holidays or for emergencies.

I'm signed up for a few survey sites myself, and I have a lot of fun doing them. Trust me, I'm not getting rich off of these! But I have been able to use the gift cards and points to get things my family needed or even just wanted. Recently, for instance, my toaster oven was dying a slow and undignified death, making us sit through three cycles before getting hot enough to actually toast. I was able to cash out the points I'd earned on MySurvey.com to get a new one, saving me from having to head out to Target to buy a replacement or from throwing my old one out the window in complete frustration. I used my Amazon.com gift cards from Valued Opinions to buy an indoor mini trampoline to keep my two active boys from going *completely* stir-crazy this past winter. This isn't something I'd necessarily have gone out and purchased at the store, but it felt like I got it for *free* because I bought it with my bonus income. Two happy, bouncing kids? Also priceless!

For more ideas on survey sites to check out, visit Engineer a Debt Free Life (www.engineeradebtfreelife.com), run by husband-and-wife bloggers. They often talk about survey sites, blog about which ones are legitimate and pay out better than others, and share their family's experiences with different sites.

GET PAID TO SEARCH

If you spend much time online, you probably spend a lot of time searching. Beyond the major search sites like Google and Yahoo!, you can use "search to win" sites that pay you for searching. The major player here is Swagbucks.com (www.swagbucks.com), which offers you the chance to earn random points, or Swag Bucks, whenever you search through Swagbucks.com or through its toolbar that you can install right on your internet browser. Search results come from Google and Ask.com and are mixed with "sponsored" results, which is how Swagbucks.com makes its money. You can then redeem your accumulated Swag Bucks for merchandise, sweepstakes entries, PayPal payments, or gift cards in the Swag Store. The biggest disadvantage is that the search results won't be as in-depth or as "good" as a Google search, so use Swagbucks.com for quick searches and a real search engine for more in-depth research.

Swagbucks.com

As already mentioned, Swagbucks.com offers a downloadable search toolbar to make it easy to remember to use its search. It also keeps users involved through Facebook (www.facebook.com/swagbucks) and Twitter (twitter.com/swagbucks)—often listing free codes on its Facebook page and Twitter feed that can be redeemed for bonus Swag Bucks. Users can also refer their friends and earn matching Swag Bucks for those their friends earn through searching, as well.

You can also sign up on sites such as BeatThat! (www.beatthat.com). Here, you can actually make money by searching for the best deals online. If you find a lower price for something than the price BeatThat! lists on its site, you get paid!

GET PAID TO VIEW ADS—AND MORE

Companies can remove the middleman by targeting consumers directly with ads and then compensating those consumers for the time it takes to view them. There are a number of players here, but they all work basically the same way. Some sites combine ad viewing with survey opportunities, and most also offer referral programs in which participants earn a sign-up bonus or a penny or two for each ad viewed by anyone they refer to the program.

You won't get rich reading ads online, but you can probably cash out for enough gift cards to buy some holiday gifts for the kids or get yourself a few lattes you wouldn't normally purchase. These sorts of online opportunities, open to anyone with an internet connection, are especially useful if you live in a rural area, where part-time work outside the home can be hard to find. The major rewards sites to sign up with include:

- CashCrate (www.cashcrate.com): Be careful with this one, as it includes "offers" on its site. Don't ever sign up for anything that requires a credit card, but if you stick to its surveys and click-throughs, you should be fine. Payout is by check, and you get bonuses for referring friends.

- Hits4Pay (www.hits4pay.com): Members need to visit the Hits4Pay site to see whether they have emails in their Hits4Pay inbox and then they get credited for reading them.

- InboxDollars (www.inboxdollars.com) and SendEarnings (www.sendearnings.com): These sister sites pay users to read emails and take surveys; refer friends and get a percentage of their earnings as well. Payout is at $30, and they give a $5 sign-up bonus.

- YouData (www.youdata.com): Complete a profile, or "MeFile," that allows advertisers to target ads to your personal interests. You then are presented with video and text ads and rewarded for watching or clicking through. The idea is that advertisers pay for your attention and are able to target their ads directly to relevant consumers. Get paid via PayPal every Friday, cash out for gift certificates to sites such as Amazon.com or iTunes, or donate your earnings to a number of charities.

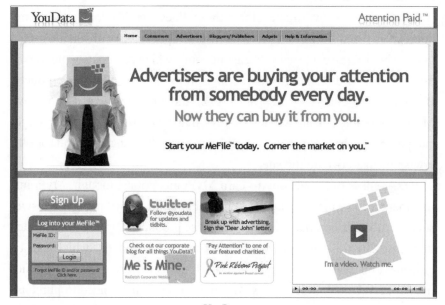

YouData

Other sites run occasional pay-per-your-view ads. You can earn discounts, magazine subscriptions, or other incentives for viewing video ads online. CVS, for example, ran an AdPerk (www.adperk.com) video rewards program in partnership with Procter & Gamble (P&G) in 2009, in which users who earned points by viewing video ads and then purchased P&G products on CVS.com received a bonus gift card. AdPerk also ran a 2009 campaign in which viewers were rewarded with free or discounted magazine subscriptions in return for a certain number of minutes watching advertising videos, and one in which viewers could get a Rite Aid coupon for watching ads. Watch for campaigns like this to become more popular. Companies know that people often skip television ads in the era of TiVo and DVR, so they are always trying new ways of getting consumers to pay attention to their messages.

Other sites to investigate along these lines are MyPoints (www.my points.com) and Reward Port (www.rewardport.com). In Chapter 6, I talked about BzzAgent (www.bzzagent.com), which recruits people to participate in word-of-mouth marketing programs for various products. Beyond the products they receive to "bzz," though, BzzAgents also receive MyPoints points for answering surveys that help BzzAgent better target campaigns, for bzzing products and reporting back on that bzz, and for otherwise being active on the site.

BzzAgent is only one way to earn MyPoints points, though. MyPoints members receive regular emails asking them to do everything from answer surveys to visit a company's site to purchase products. Participating in each of these activities earns members a set amount of points, which can be redeemed on MyPoints for prizes and gift cards to various stores, including Amazon.com and Starbucks. You don't ever actually need to purchase anything to earn points on MyPoints; you can earn points simply by clicking through on these daily emails.

Reward Port works in a similar way: You earn points by answering surveys, shopping online, and completing offers. (In this case, "offers" can sometimes be as innocuous as signing up for a company's online newsletter. As always, read what you're agreeing to before signing up for anything!) You can redeem these points for gift cards to stores ranging from Amazon.com to Target to Starbucks.

Reward Port

Get Paid to Complete Tasks

Some sites also pay real human beings to complete tasks that just can't be completely automated. Sign up with Amazon.com's Mechanical Turk (www.mturk.com/mturk/welcome) to see thousands of HITs (Human Intelligence Tasks) for you to choose from. Browse through the HITs and pick and complete those of interest; when the requester approves your work, payment will be deposited into your Amazon.com payments account. While most HITs pay only a few cents, most can be completed very quickly, so this is a fun option to earn a little extra cash when you have a bit of downtime. You can also complete "qualifications" to see additional HITs (often somewhat higher paying) that are only available to qualified Mechanical Turk workers.

You can also try completing tasks on Mahalo (www.mahalo.com/tasks). These pay out varying amounts of "Mahalo dollars," and once you hit a

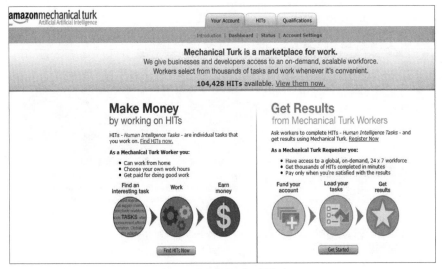

Amazon's Mechanical Turk

certain amount, you can request that these be deposited into your PayPal account. (At the time of this writing, each Mahalo dollar is worth 75 cents in U.S. dollars.) Also on Mahalo, you can write search result pages at Mahalo Greenhouse (greenhouse.mahalo.com). These human-created and -reviewed search pages become part of the Mahalo human-powered search engine (www.mahalo.com).

Lastly, check out DoMyStuff.com (www.domystuff.com). People and businesses post tasks they need done—anything from dog walking to lawn mowing to web design—and then you can "bid" on those tasks. You'll need to pay DoMyStuff.com 25 cents to get the contact information for each "employer," which is probably why fewer tasks are listed here, but it's an interesting idea to check out.

GET PAID TO ANSWER QUESTIONS

While Google is great, sometimes people just want an answer from a human being, or they have a question Google can't resolve. If you're an expert in certain areas, or if you're great at tracking down information, think about signing up to answer questions from other internet users. These expert answer sites include:

- ChaCha (becomeaguide.chacha.com): Answer questions from ChaCha users and get paid on a per-transaction basis. ChaCha says that most Guides earn $3 to $9 per hour, paid via debit card or direct deposit. According to the ChaCha site, "Guides may be Generalists skilled at navigating the Web, Specialists with lots of passion and knowledge on a particular topic, Expeditors with a knack for fast-paced puzzle solving, or Transcribers who make ChaCha the smartest voice service in the world."

- JustAnswer.com (www.justanswer.com/expert.aspx): Choose a category from its list and sign up to become an expert on the site. You'll get 25 percent to 50 percent of what customers offer for each answer, paid via PayPal once you hit $20.

- LivePerson (www.liveperson.com/registration/expert-registration/expert-signup.aspx): Sign up to get listed in your area of personal expertise, and then LivePerson clients can find you and ask you questions via live chat. You set your own per-minute rate, and LivePerson takes a commission.

- Mahalo Answers (www.mahalo.com/answers): As when you complete Mahalo tasks, answering questions on Mahalo earns you Mahalo dollars, which you can eventually turn into PayPal payments.

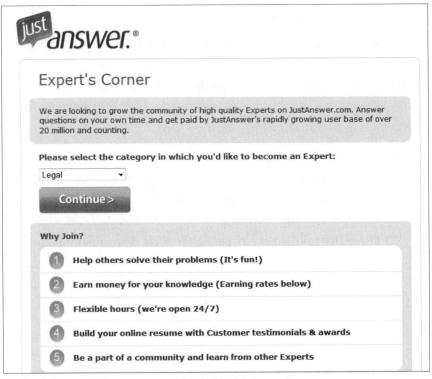

JustAnswer.com

You'll do best on some of these sites if you're already an expert in a certain area. Were you once a lawyer, doctor, or electrician, for instance? Share your knowledge with others. While this is usually side income, the flexibility of these sites (you log in and answer questions whenever you have spare time) lets you work around your kids' schedules. And it can be fun! You can exercise your brain and learn new things while earning some money!

Any of these extra income opportunities mashes up well with your new-found savings strategies. If you've found ways to reduce your grocery budget, then the dollars you earn online go much, much further. If you're looking at Amazon.com and other sites for deals, then the gift cards you earn online can give you a very nice Christmas. This is where everything you're doing starts to click: You're really a *mashup mom* when you combine your money-saving and money-making activities in the right balance to make it all work for you!

9

Organization, Balance, and Planning

Now that you're thinking about how best to juggle your money-saving and money-making strategies, it's time to think about how they mash up with your bigger life goals as you plan for your future. It's also time to think about how best to organize your life and your resources to take advantage of the opportunities in front of you. One of the things I've learned on this mashed-up journey is that using online resources to make and save money doesn't just help in the short term. Saving money on your everyday essentials *now* lets you put more aside for long-term goals. Saving time *now* lets you devote more time to your family and to thinking about how to achieve your long-term goals.

Getting in the mind-set of saving and making money whenever possible is also the first step toward developing the mind-set you need to begin living within your means, paying off your debt, and planning for the future. Seeing how small savings add up can really be the incentive you need in order to extend these savings further! A lot of online resources also help us save for the future, from online banks that tend to offer higher interest rates than your local bank might to college savings programs that offer money back on everyday purchases. Here, I want to talk about some that have been particularly useful to me in terms of planning ahead, including resources that can help you see what you might need to put aside for retirement and how your short-term spending decisions affect your long-term goals.

Focusing on the future also means that it's time to think about your *own* long-term goals, financial and otherwise. You might be a stay-at-home or work-at-home mom now, but what do you see yourself doing in 5 years? In 10? Our working careers far outlast our time home with our kids, and we need to think about what will prepare us to move forward when we're ready to take that step. You might be at home or scaled back right now because of the economy, but where do you see yourself going when economic conditions improve? This is one reason to continue with income-earning activities while at home: The more you've done, the more attractive you'll be to potential employers if and when you decide to re-enter the full-time workforce.

As I've said before, frugality at its heart requires planning ahead. We just can't be frugal if we're always buying things on impulse—or running out of items and having to pay full price. The end of the mashup mom journey focuses on strategies to simplify the ways you organize your work life, home life, and savings for optimal effectiveness, for you and for your family. As always, you can use technology to help find balance. While for many of us technology unfortunately seems to complicate our lives, when we use it strategically, it can really help simplify many of our everyday activities.

In Her Own Words

Melody C. is a stay-at-home mom.

My parents had eight kids, and even though Dad was not a college grad, they stretched their money to amazing lengths through couponing and refunding and not spending money they didn't have. So I was raised on this lifestyle. However, the internet has brought a lot of change to couponing, and refunding has generally dwindled. I got reintroduced to the "new couponing" when my girlfriend invited our MOMS Club chapter to attend one of Jill Cataldo's couponing classes. Since I grew up in the South and only moved to Illinois in 2006, I had a lot to learn about local stores and their policies. I took the class in November, and by January I was seeing major savings in my budget.

The one area that we spent the most money on with the least long-term value was food. I used to spend $500 to $600 on groceries and $200 on eating out every month. One month I realized we had spent over $800 on food and thought we had to make a change! Once I learned how to best work the deals at our local stores and we finally had a house, I started seriously stockpiling. As a result, as of the last 3 months I am now spending $150 to $200 a month on groceries. We've been able to make big donations to our local charities every month on that amount as well. This is saving me approximately $4,800 a year on grocery and household items.

My coupon savings allowed me to increase our excess (payments beyond the required minimum payments) debt repayment from $900 a month to $1,300 a month. This has made a huge difference in our timeline for our financial goals. I figured out that we could have our car loans and credit cards paid off in 6 months! Then, I looked at how paying extra on our [house] could shorten our 30-year mortgage.

If you take all 30 years to pay off your mortgage loan, even on our 5.5 percent fixed-rate mortgage, you will end up paying for two homes, due to the amount of interest you pay over the life of the loan. That's got to hurt! After we pay off our other debts, if we include both the required minimum payments we have been making on the mortgage, plus that extra $1,300, we will be able to pay off our mortgage faster. At that rate, our 30-year mortgage would be paid off in less than 9 years!! Can you imagine *owning* your own home with *no mortgage* payment, only 9 years after you bought it? For a family that had only 3 percent to put down to begin with, this really makes our hearts race. Realizing this has made us very committed to keeping on track with our budget— and using coupons to make it happen!

We also like to save for presents all year round in an interest-bearing savings account so Christmas isn't such a burden. We have huge families, and this has made quite a difference in paying cash for Christmas instead of plying the credit cards with debt. We buy used toys and clothes for our son at various resale events. This has reduced our clothing and present budgets tremendously. He gets more toys and clothes than ever at a fraction of the cost that we would have spent on these items if we had bought them new at the store. It's August, and I have his birthday [gifts], Christmas [gifts], and a huge fall-winter wardrobe sitting in our attic ready and waiting for him.

This year, I'm finding lots of deals on gifts through couponing as well. I may not need that gift fund this year, and it can keep growing the interest for next year. Any big purchase gets a savings account, including when we were ready to start trying to have our first child. Want a new car? Start a car fund. We also have an emergency fund that we are increasing to cover 6 months of expenses. It's not a matter of if, but when something unexpected will happen.

ORGANIZE YOUR TIME

Organizing your time can take a number of forms and can save you money and effort in multiple ways. Do you remember when the price of gas spiked to unheard-of levels in 2008, and you were advised to combine trips as much as possible? Well, just as you did then, combine activities to get done what you need to do while wasting as little time as possible. Just as when you're saving or earning, even little changes here add up to save you time, effort, and money. For instance, if you're "cherry-picking" those deals at multiple stores, plan your route so that you can do so efficiently in one outing, or on your way home from work, school, or other commitments. Your time is valuable, so maximize it!

Take small steps to start. Get yourself on the "do not call" list to cut down drastically on time-wasting (and annoying) telemarketing calls to your home (www.donotcall.gov). Check out DMAchoice (www.dma choice.org) to do something similar with direct mail; you can opt out of various categories such as credit card offers, catalogs, and more. Take the time to plan menus around store sales and your stockpiles each week. This will not only help you organize your shopping trips, but it will help you organize your time when you're not scrambling for last-minute dinner ideas. Think of all the little ways you can simplify your life and your daily activities, and try implementing one a week; see how they add up!

ORGANIZE YOUR COUPONS

Because there are so many ways to find and use coupons, you can see that once you start the coupon clipping-printing-snagging habit, you will soon find you have more than you can deal with by simply throwing them in a drawer or into your purse. There's nothing more aggravating than finding out that a batch of good coupons you had been meaning to use had expired or trying to plan a shopping trip and being unable to find the coupons you

just *know* you have somewhere. To save yourself time and aggravation, you
need to get organized—and fast! Different people have different methods
of organizing, but they tend to boil down to four main systems.

System 1: The clipless system. When you get the Sunday paper each
week, don't cut the coupons out of the inserts. Instead, write the date on the
front of each insert with permanent marker and slide the insert into a file
folder ordered by date. You can then use online coupon databases to locate
which Sunday insert(s) particular coupons appeared in when you're writing up your shopping list each week. Deal bloggers also will tell you which
date and which insert that the coupons appeared in, so if you follow them
to plan your shopping trips, they'll keep you in the know. This system saves
you time up front, but its disadvantage lies in the fact that many of your
coupons will be at home when you run across an unadvertised deal at the
store.

System 2: The clip everything, alphabetical file system. Clip everything,
and file coupons alphabetically by product behind alphabetical tabs in a
box or in an accordion folder. This allows you to easily see if you have a
coupon for Product X when a sale comes along.

System 3: The clip everything, category-based file system. Clip everything, and file coupons by category in a coupon box or in an accordion
folder. Your categories will vary according to your family's needs, but you
might, for instance, have categories such as "baby," "dairy," and "frozen."
Some people make up their own broad categories, while others categorize
their coupons in the same way products are arranged in their favorite local
grocery store.

System 4: The clip everything binder system. Clip everything and file
coupons in baseball card (or other plastic) holders inside a three-ring zipper binder. This allows you to tote the whole binder along to the store, so
you aren't caught without coupons when you find a clearance sale or

unadvertised deal. Back-to-school sales are a great time to find a deal on a zipper binder!

If you choose to use a clipless system—or even if you just want to check whether there are coupons out there—you'll want to bookmark some online coupon databases. The biggest coupon databases are CouponTom.com (www.coupontom.com) and Hot Coupon World (www.hotcouponworld.com/forums/coupon.php, which includes an expired coupon database, if any of your local stores take these). Remember, though, that some coupons are regional. You may not find every coupon these databases list in your own inserts or the values may differ.

CouponTom.com
quickly find grocery coupons

| Coupon Search | Price Book | Weekly Ads | Insert Schedule | Tools |

Start typing to find a coupon

cheerios

Search through thousands of grocery coupons found in your Sunday paper, All You magazine and across the internet.

SHARE

Location	Expires	Description	Discount	Qty	
08-02 S2	Sep 12	General Mills Frosted Cheerios , Fruity Cheerios, Apple Cinnamon Cheerios, Banana Nut Cheerios or Yogurt Burst Cheerios Cereal any	$1.00	2	Clip
08-16 S	Sep 26	General Mills Frosted Cheerios , Fruity Cheerios, Apple Cinnamon Cheerios, Banana Nut Cheerios or Yogurt Burst Cheerios , Original, Honey Nut, Berry Burst Cheerios, MultiGrain or Cheerios crunch Cereal any	$1.00	2	Clip
08-09 GM	Oct 03	General Mills Cheerios Snack Mix any size/flavor	$0.50	1	Clip

Search for "Cheerios" on CouponTom.com

Use these databases to look up a product and find out what insert you can find coupons in and for what amount. Here, you'll need to know some abbreviations:

- AY stands for *All You* magazine, available at Walmart and by subscription. Because it includes so many coupons—and so many people subscribe *just* for the coupons—most databases now include it in their listings.

- GM stands for General Mills, which offers the occasional special coupon insert for its products.

- K stands for Kellogg's, which puts out a special back-to-school coupon insert at the end of the summer.

- PG stands for Procter & Gamble, which produces a monthly coupon insert for its products.

- RP stands for RedPlum, which appears in many Sunday papers. You might also see R1 and R2 for weeks that included multiple RedPlum inserts.

- S or SS stands for SmartSource, which appears in many Sunday papers. You might also see S1 and S2 for weeks that included multiple SmartSource inserts.

- U stands for Unilever, which puts out the occasional insert with coupons for its own brands.

- V stands for Valassis, the same as RedPlum.

For instance, if you see 5/31 S1 listed when you look up a product, it means that a coupon for it can be found in the first SmartSource coupon insert on May 31.

If you're intimidated by the organization process, you can also purchase complete coupon organization systems online. The main two are TheCouponBinder.com (www.thecouponbinder.com) and The Couponizer (www.couponizer.com). Don't want to pay for the convenience? Study what they're offering and pick up the separate components at your local store.

ORGANIZE YOUR STOCKPILE

Once you start buying extra items at their lowest price, you will need to organize them so that you don't lose track of what you have or think you've run out of something that's just been shoved to the back of the shelf. Be sure to sort your items so that those with the soonest expiration date are toward the front, because you'll want to use these first. If you see that an item is nearing its expiration date and you won't be able to use it, donate it to the food pantry. Donated food goes quickly and will be used quickly. Also, keep like items together for easy accessibility and seeing at a glance what you have. You might want to buy some shelving or find another way to keep items organized and easily visible.

Organizing your stockpile helps you plan your meals and shopping trips. When you're able to quickly see what you have, you're able to plan meals around your stockpile. You also are less likely to purchase duplicate items—you don't want to get home and find that you already have eight boxes of cereal, but they've just been shoved to the back of the closet under a pile of clothes.

SAVE TIME WITH TECHNOLOGY ON THE GO

Once you've started to get organized, you can save time when you're out and about, too! We often need information about deals, coupons, or commitments on-the-go, when it's just not convenient to get behind a computer. Enter mobile apps! As smartphones become increasingly popular (if

An organized stockpile

perhaps not exactly frugal), we can find more and more money- and time-saving applications, or apps, for these devices. Now, because we can be online wherever we are, we can find deals and maximize our time and our savings wherever we are. I already talked about some ways to load coupons onto your cell phone, but you can take advantage of your phone's capabilities in other ways as well.

And, sometimes, just the simplest functions can be the most useful—I use the calculator on my iPhone on almost every grocery outing to make sure I'm adding things up right at the store or to figure out per-unit costs that aren't clearly marked. Yes, there's math involved in saving, but that's *why* they invented calculators. I highly recommend carrying a little one from the dollar store in your purse if you don't have a calculator on your phone. Regardless, if you're going to be paying that cell phone bill each month, make sure you get your money's worth out of it. Here are some ideas.

Texting: It's Not Just for Teenagers Anymore

One newer couponing development is the ability to receive coupons and coupon codes by text message to your mobile device. (Before trying this, make sure you have a phone plan that includes texting so that you don't get dinged with charges both ways for texts!) Redbox (www.redbox.com), for example, often releases coupon codes via text—you text a word or phrase to a given number, and Redbox texts you back with a code for a free movie rental. Redbox also runs a free movie Monday service; sign up to receive a code via text for a free rental on the first Monday of every month. TGI Friday's (www.fridays.com) has been releasing coupons you can either print or receive on your mobile phone when you text.

Some companies will also let you sign up to receive free samples via text message. Here's how it works: You'll usually text a special code to a given number, then receive a message back with instructions for sending your mailing address. Again, because these require several back-and-forth messages, be sure you aren't paying per text. Services such as ShopText (www.shoptext.com) let you sign up to receive samples, get coupons, and enter sweepstakes on your mobile phone. Ads and posters with the ShopText logo let you shop and request samples just by using the code found in the ad.

You can also use services such as Frucall (www.frucall.com) to comparison shop when you're out and about. When you see a sale in a store but aren't sure whether you could get a better deal at another store or online, you can call, text, or enter a barcode on Frucall's mobile site to compare prices elsewhere. You can make purchases right through Frucall or save items and prices to explore later. Given the ever-increasing popularity of texting, the use of these sorts of services is sure to grow.

Mobile Apps

If you have a smartphone, you'll want to look into mobile apps that can help you save and organize. I'll list just a few examples because there are literally hundreds to choose from. Search in the iPhone app store or search online to find additional apps that meet your own needs. Your mobile organizational apps or built-in tools such as calendars and to-do lists can also be extremely valuable because they let you track what you're doing and enter new commitments wherever you are. (No more scribbling on little scraps of paper and trying to remember to run to the calendar as soon as you get home!)

Mobile apps for price comparison and deals allow you to find the best prices and grab coupons wherever you are. For instance, Yowza!! (www.get yowza.com), which is free for the iPhone (or iPod Touch), was cofounded by Greg Grunberg of *Heroes*; it uses your current geographic location to push deal alerts and on-screen coupons to you for stores in your area. Cashiers can scan the coupon bar codes right from your iPhone screen.

You can also look into personal finance apps. Mint.com (www.mint.com), for instance, offers an iPhone app that allows you to keep track of your personal finances wherever you are. In the store? See whether a large purchase will put you over budget or whether your paycheck has cleared yet so that you don't incur overdraft feeds. This app syncs with your personal bank accounts, so you always get real-time updates.

Other apps fill different niches. Several, for instance, focus on organic and green products. The Environmental Working Group (www.foodnews.org) has an iPhone app that you can use while shopping to see what types of produce are most important to buy organic and what conventionally grown fruits and vegetables are OK to buy if organic isn't available or is too pricey. T-Mobile offers a downloadable app for its customers that gives you coupons for "green" products (www.mobilizewitht-mobile.com/mobilize-shop-green-perks.aspx).

Apps from your favorite stores allow you to load coupons, compare prices, and see deals. Some also will load coupons for you to redeem in store by showing the cashier a numerical code or scannable bar code on your screen. Search your app store or search online to see which of your favorites make these available. As with texting, these types of services are likely to grow in popularity, so keep that in mind when it's time to upgrade or replace your mobile phone. While you can take advantage of a number of deals with simple text technology, the ability to display coupons on screen and to run apps is becoming more and more important.

ORGANIZE YOUR FINANCES

Organizing your finances, of course, could be a whole book in itself. But I just want to tell you about some useful online tools that help you get a visual picture of where your money is going, get support from others, and find tools to help you manage your money. You'll also want to know your credit score and get your credit reports, so be sure to request your free credit reports annually at AnnualCreditReport.com (www.annualcredit report.com). Use this site, not the ones you see advertised on TV; those are a scam that try to get you to pay for information to which you are freely entitled. To get your credit, or FICO, score, check out Credit Karma (www.creditkarma.com).

Other sites offer a useful—and sometimes humorous—look at saving and personal finance, helping remove some of the intimidation factor around these topics. Here are some of my favorites:

- Choose to Save (www.choosetosave.org): Helps you take the steps you need in order to save and prepare for retirement.

- Feed the Pig (www.feedthepig.org): Specifically targets 25- to 34-year-olds but is useful for anyone. Use its interactive calculators to find out how little changes can add up to big savings and see visuals depicting the impact of your spending habits.

- Geezeo (www.geezeo.com): This social financial site is like Weight Watchers for personal finance. Get motivated by being in it together with others, plus get advice from experts. Use the site's tools to create a budget and set financial goals. One interesting twist is the chance to make financial confessions—get them off your chest here so you can move on!

- Green Sherpa (www.greensherpa.com): Lets you manage all your accounts together so you can get a more accurate picture of your cash flow and net worth. Green Sherpa helps you track your spending and project spending 12 months out so that you can see the effects of your buying patterns.

- Mint.com (www.mint.com): Mint.com has so many tools that it's hard to even list them all. Start here to get a solid look at personal finance and use interactive tools. Mint.com also has a nice online tool that helps you find lower-rate credit cards, a good step to take while you're paying off debt to help you get out of the hole sooner.

- Wesabe (www.wesabe.com): Somewhat like Geezeo, Wesabe combines a social networking site and tools to organize and to track your finances into one. Getting support and feedback from others in an online community can help you feel less alone and get useful advice on moving forward.

Several of these personal finance resources have learned from and built on social networking sites. They help you tap into the power of community to help you stay on track. Others just give you the tools you need to easily organize your budget, personal finances, and savings strategies.

Mint.com

SAVE FOR THE FUTURE

While in the past you might just have chosen to deposit your money at the closest local bank, you can now choose from a number of online competitors to help you more save more money easily. Avoid banks with excessive or unnecessary fees, which can really add up. Online savings accounts tend to offer higher interest rates and some interesting flexibility. The most popular online banks include:

- EmigrantDirect (www.emigrantdirect.com)

- ING Direct (www.ingdirect.com)

- HSBC (www.hsbc.com)

Some of these offer useful options such as children's online savings accounts and family financial planning or accounts with no fees and no minimums (which allows you to set up several smaller separate accounts to save toward specific goals). Online savings accounts are also useful in that they make it more difficult to blow money on impulse purchases because you have to wait a day or two for a transfer to clear into your regular checking account!

You might also think about automating your savings by setting up an automatic weekly transfer from your main checking account to an online bank with a higher interest rate. Set it up for just $20 or $25 a week, and you might not even notice the difference, but you will see the savings build up. (Just be sure to record these transfers so that you know what you have in checking!) When you make bonus money on the side through online activities or freelancing and you don't need that income to live on, deposit it directly into an online account so that you never see (or spend) it. As Wyoming librarian Laura C. suggests, "I do a very small amount of freelance writing in addition to my regular job. I now put all the money that I make from freelance writing (and all the mileage reimbursement checks and other odd bits of unexpected money that I get) straight into my savings account, on the theory that they aren't part of my regular paycheck, and that if I put them away immediately, I won't notice they're missing—and won't spend them on trivia."

If you're saving for a specific goal (e.g., a car, a vacation), you can check out SmartyPig (www.smartypig.com). Set up an account there to save for something specific and then set up recurring contributions to that account. You can choose to make your account "public," so that family and friends can see your progress, lend you moral support, and even contribute if they want. This can be a great way to answer the "what do you want for your birthday" question! It's free to set up an account and withdraw funds, and your SmartyPig goal accounts do earn interest.

SmartyPig

Little changes such as switching to paying bills online can also save you both time and money. With first-class stamps up to 44 cents each and likely to jump again, most households spend at least $5 a month in postage for bills alone (not to mention the cost of checks and your time in writing and mailing them). Save more than $60 a year—not to mention a lot of time and energy—by switching to online bill pay. Most banks offer this as a free option with their checking accounts, and once you've set up payee listings for your monthly bills, it takes very little time to go online and make these payments. While $60 a year doesn't sound like much, little things *do* add up. Put it toward internet access, go out for a nice birthday dinner, or buy a big birthday gift for one of your kids. And when you do write checks, get cheaper check refills than your bank usually offers by going to Checks Unlimited (www.checksunlimited.com) or Checks in the Mail (www.checksinthemail.com).

You can compare interest rates among various checking and savings accounts—as well as money market and CD rates—at Bankrate.com (www.bankrate.com). Again, you're no longer locked into what your local banks offer. Just transfer money online when you need to and take advantage of the best possible rates. Especially when interest rates are so low, every little bit helps! MoneyAisle (www.moneyaisle.com) offers an interesting twist on this. You can enter your information to find high interest savings accounts or CDs, and banks bid in live auctions for your business. If you prefer to stay with a local bank or want a local checking account in addition to an online savings account, find the best checking account rates near you at CheckingFinder.com (www.checkingfinder.com).

SAVE FOR COLLEGE

If you have children and are thinking ahead to how much college is going to cost by the time they attend school, or if you are planning on going back at some point, you'll want to look into online resources to help you save and strategize. You can also look into programs that give cash back for everyday purchases. These work similarly to the online rebate sites discussed in Chapter 5, but these programs deposit rebates into college savings instead of into a rebate account.

$$$ *Upromise* $$$

We signed up for Upromise (www.upromise.com) shortly after my first son was born, and I'm so glad we did. The looming cost of college for two kids scares the heck out of me, and any little bit helps! Here's the deal: When you join Upromise, you save for college by making everyday purchases. Register your store loyalty cards and your credit cards, then get rebates into your Upromise account for dining at participating restaurants, shopping online at participating merchants, purchasing plane tickets online, buying participating products using your store loyalty card, and so on.

In addition to the automatic savings you receive from purchasing participating products, Upromise offers monthly ecoupons you can load onto your Upromise account. These are often a double dip with other manufacturer or electronic store coupons, allowing you to save money when you buy the product, then save extra for college.

The money you accumulate in your Upromise account can all go to one beneficiary or be split between beneficiaries. You can link your account to some participating 529 accounts or withdraw funds from Upromise and deposit them in your own 529 account. Your friends and family can also sign up to save toward the same beneficiary, if grandparents, aunts, or godparents want to play along.

I know it's easy to procrastinate about setting up something like this. But really, once you sign up and get those cards registered, you don't have to change your shopping habits. Just look at anything you earn through Upromise as a bonus; don't buy things just because of their participation in Upromise. And because it doesn't cost anything to sign up except for the bit of time it takes to register your cards, why the heck not? We all have to shop, and we all have to eat, so why not get something back for our kids?

Is this going to pay for college in and of itself? No, but it will allow you to put more into a 529 plan than you would otherwise be able to; it's basically free money. And who doesn't like that?

You can also use sites such as BabyMint (www.babymint.com) to get rebates from participating retailers and service providers. While the BabyMint network is somewhat smaller than Upromise's, this money can be deposited directly into your 529 or Coverdell college savings account, disbursed by check, or paid toward college loans. BabyMint also has a nifty Tuition Rewards program (www.babymint.com/Info/NFO_Tuition Rewards.aspx) that's redeemable at more than 175 colleges and universities—basically, your savings are matched with an equal tuition break at a participating school. There are a number of restrictions on this program and you have to enter early, so read about it at the BabyMint site to see whether it will work for you.

Some financial institutions offer credit cards that will deposit rebates into your 529 account with them. Check with your bank to see what it might have available.

Upromise

Financial Aid and Loans

Beyond helping you save for college, the internet offers a multitude of resources to help you pay for college. Here, as always, it can be difficult to sort out the most useful and legitimate sites, so let me take a stab at it for you. Here are just a very few:

- FastWeb (www.fastweb.com): Search for scholarships by many different criteria.

- FinAid (www.finaid.org): Find everything you need to know about saving for college, from savings plans to loans and scholarship search (through FastWeb). Also includes useful calculators for everything from college costs to what your family will be expected to contribute.

- Savingforcollege.com (www.savingforcollege.com): Use one of this site's most useful features and compare the performance of various 529 college savings plans. Because these plans are one of the most popular and important ways of saving for college, get the info you need here.

- SimpleTuition (www.simpletuition.com): Find private and federal loans.

You can also compare student loan rates and find information on saving and paying for college at Bankrate.com (www.bankrate.com/student-loans.aspx). And if you or your kids are struggling to pay back student loans, think about consolidating your government loans. Find out more at Direct Consolidation Loans (loanconsolidation.ed.gov).

Get Kids Involved

Get kids involved in saving for their own future, whether or not that includes college. It's never too early, and this helps lay the foundation for being responsible for their own income and earnings throughout their life. If you get them involved throughout the whole mashup mom process, the idea of saving in all areas of life should start to become natural to them.

Since you want to get your whole family involved in saving money, the whole family can also be involved in earning money—and part of that money can be earmarked for college funds. Teens can babysit, mow lawns, find a part-time job at their local fast-food place, bag groceries, serve as camp counselors, and otherwise start bringing in their own income. Tell them they need to earn their own gas money, pay their own cell phone bill, or use their own money for extras, and that should be a good motivator.

Having their own income helps them learn to make wiser financial decisions; money always means more if it's not handed to you. Teens should also check out Myfirstpaycheck.com (www.myfirstpaycheck.com), a site devoted entirely to job listings for teens.

Peer-to-Peer Lending

Peer-to-peer lending is an interesting concept. Some newer sites allow you to invest your money by loaning it to other actual people. Prosper (www.prosper.com), although currently available only in certain states, is the main player here. (Lenders on Prosper are actually technically making an investment, and there is a risk, as always, of losing your initial investment. Do your research when deciding which loans to fund.) As a Prosper lender, you receive monthly payments (with interest) into your account as borrowers repay their loans.

If you would rather invest in someone's education, check out GreenNote (www.greennote.com). Through GreenNote, you can lend funds to a student you know, to a student at your own alma mater, or to a student in your community. You can search for students by many characteristics and lend only to someone you believe in.

Also check out MicroPlace (www.microplace.com), an eBay-owned organization that connects investors with microfinance (small-loan) institutions looking for funds. Your investment here can help others around the globe lift themselves out of poverty—and you earn interest! Your minimum investment here is just $20, so it's worth looking into. Your return on your investment ranges from 0.5 percent to 6 percent.

No-Fee and Rewards Credit Cards

Although it's become more difficult to qualify for a credit card lately and rates have gone up, credit is still available, and the situation may improve.

MicroPlace

If you're going to be using a credit card at all, you want to find a no-fee card that offers you rewards on everyday purchases. *Assuming you are paying off the balance each month*, these are wonderful to use in conjunction with rebate sites or with Upromise. You can get one rebate back into college savings from Upromise or into your online rebate account, then get a second rebate through your credit card company. Just as you stack savings at the store, you can also stack cash back from multiple places.

Bankrate.com (www.bankrate.com/credit-cards.aspx) lets you compare credit card interest rates, fees, and features. Also try CardRatings.com (www.cardratings.com) to compare hundreds of credit cards—complete with real people's reviews. And BillShrink (www.billshrink.com) offers a handy interactive site that lets you input your shopping habits, monthly purchase amount, and preferences to find the credit card that best fits your shopping pattern and will maximize your rewards.

If you've gotten yourself into trouble with credit cards in the past, you still may want to have one, at least for emergencies, and because not having a credit card at all can affect your credit rating. Use the freezer trick if necessary: Literally freeze your credit card inside a block of ice to force yourself to seriously consider whether to use it for a purchase. Never buy anything if you're not sure you can make the payment in full at the end of the month.

Using credit wisely by charging only what you know you can pay off in full each month helps you build a good credit rating and can pay off in rewards points. I use an Amazon.com Visa for all my online purchases and travel expenses. It pays me in Amazon.com gift certificates every time I charg a certain dollar amount. For our other everyday purchases, we use Discover, which gives a percentage back in cash or in gift cards to various stores. As always, do this *only for purchases you're going to be making anyway and have the cash to pay for.* If it's something you'd otherwise buy with cash, you can buy it with a credit card, get the rebate, and *save the cash* specifically to pay off the credit card at the end of the month.

Focus on *Your* Future

At some point on this journey, you will ask yourself, where to from here? Regularly take stock of your situation and your strategies. Ask yourself a few questions to make sure you're on track: Is your at-home situation stopgap, or is it career building? Do you want to investigate additional money-making opportunities, or is it time to look for part- or full-time employment out of the home? Are your money-saving strategies working for you, or are there places you need to tweak them? Are you moving toward your goals or falling behind?

Above all, remember that you can carry your money-saving ways throughout your life, and you can use online resources to remain connected and active so that you're ready to move forward at the next stage of your life. I really like a site called Encore (www.encore.org), which focuses on "encore careers," or finding meaningful work for the second half of your life. If you've taken some time out of the full-time, paid workforce to care for children or others, how do you now plan for the rest of your career?

One way to think ahead is by exploring different skills with online classes and tutorials. Learnthat.com (www.learnthat.com) is a great place to find online tutorials on everything from investing to Adobe Dreamweaver. Think about the skills that you want to sharpen, things you've always wanted to learn, or what will be useful to you in your next career, then look for ways to build those skills online. If you want to get ambitious, why not access the content of almost every Massachusetts Institute of Technology (MIT) course (not for credit) at MIT OpenCourse Ware (ocw.mit.edu)?

Change Your Thinking

One joy of changing the way you save and earn money lies in giving yourself more freedom. It may give you the freedom to work for yourself. It may give you the freedom to stay in the paid workforce by earning money from home, avoiding the career gaps that hurt women when they try to re-enter the workforce. It may give you the freedom to plan your life flexibly around your responsibilities to your family. It may give you the freedom to use your hard-won dollars on more fun or fruitful pursuits than paying inflated prices for everyday essentials.

Your priorities, though, will change as your kids get older and your family responsibilities shift. Realize that these money-saving and money-making strategies can carry through even if you eventually decide to move back into the outside workforce. You can have a full-time or part-time day job *and* earn money on the side. You can work *and* clip coupons. Why not? As you get more confident in your money-saving, money-making strategies, these start to become second nature, giving you the freedom and time to combine them with other activities.

As I've mentioned before, this isn't a book on personal finance or paying down debt, although the money-saving and money-making strategies you pick up should help you do so over time. If you are ready to take that next step and start getting serious about personal finance and getting out of debt, though, there are some fantastic online resources to help you get started. Here are some of my favorites:

- Get Rich Slowly (www.getrichslowly.org/blog): The site's tagline? "Personal finance that makes cents"—and it surely does! Clear and easy-to-read posts address every aspect of personal finance, from choosing a bank account to saving at the store by growing your own vegetables.

- The Simple Dollar (www.thesimpledollar.com): The tagline here? "Financial talk for the rest of us." This is another blog that puts personal finance into understandable terms. The author's "reader mailbag" feature is fun, too. He regularly answers questions from actual readers.

- I Will Teach You to Be Rich (www.iwillteachyoutoberich.com): This blog focuses on personal finance and entrepreneurship—in very blunt terms.

- Dave Ramsey (www.daveramsey.com): Ramsey, author of the bestselling *The Total Money Makeover*, helps people get out of debt and get their finances in order.

When you start following these blogs and sites, you'll find the ones that best fit you. Follow links to other personal finance bloggers and experts, and, just as with deal blogs and work-at-home forums, you'll find your own personal finance "home" online.

STEP BACK AND SEE THE PROCESS

We've come a long way now, so let's take a step back and think about the mashup mom process! Remember, mashup moms combine money-saving and money-making strategies, finding the right balance for their own family and to help weather tough economic times. Here's the step-by-step process in a nutshell.

1. *Change your attitude toward frugality.* Remember: Frugal does *not* mean cheap, and it doesn't have to be excessive to be effective.

2. *Get online and get connected.* Find the right online fit for you, choose at least a blogger or two to follow, and find support from others going through the same things.

3. *Change the way you shop.* Think about changing your bad shopping habits and about the best ways to plan your savings.

4. *Maximize your grocery and drugstore savings.* Learn how to use coupons effectively, where to find them, and how to combine strategies to get the most out of your trips.

5. *Move online for savings.* Get discounts on everything, find reviews of products and services, and use the internet for everything from entertainment to restaurant reservations to telephone service.

6. *Find freebies for fun.* We all need a pick-me-up, especially when we're trying to make it in a down economy. Refresh your spirits with online freebies.

7. *Make money from home.* Think about ways you can use your skills and knowledge in your own freelance career or home-based business.

8. *Make money on the side.* Earn some bonus income through everyday online activities.

9. *Organize your life and plan for the future.* Get it all together and think about what's next!

WHAT'S NEXT?

There's no telling what's in store for the future of online money-saving and money-making opportunities. When the first coupon forums sprang up years ago, no one could have predicted the rise of Facebook, Twitter, and mobile apps or the explosion of blogs. When people first started telecommuting, no one could have predicted the way in which online tools make it both simple and natural. It does seem safe to say that mobile apps and coupons will only rise in popularity; both companies and consumers appreciate the convenience—and it kills fewer trees! Almost 20 percent of Americans now access the internet daily via a mobile device, and manufacturers are surely paying attention to these numbers.

As we watch for the next big thing, we can be comfortable in the fact that stores and manufacturers compete for our attention and our shopping dollars and this is only good for consumers in the long run.

And what's next for you? Only you can answer that. But if you continue to mash up these strategies, it's sure to be interesting! So get out there and plan to mash up your own ways to save and make money. I look forward to hearing more about your journey at MashupMom.com.

Recommended Reading

While the websites listed throughout this book could keep you busy for years, sometimes you just want to settle in with a good book. Here are some I've found to be useful in my own journey.

10,001 Ways to Live Large on a Small Budget. New York: Skyhorse Publishing, 2009.

Alboher, Marci. *One Person/Multiple Careers: A New Model for Work/Life Success.* New York: Warner, 2007.

Barr, Tracy. *Living Well in a Down Economy for Dummies.* New York: Wiley, 2008.

Economides, Steve and Annette. *America's Cheapest Family Gets You Right on the Money: Your Guide to Living Better, Spending Less, and Cashing in on Your Dreams.* New York: Three Rivers Press, 2007.

Edwards, Paul, and Sarah Edwards. *Secrets of Self-Employment: Surviving and Thriving on the Ups and Downs of Being Your Own Boss.* New York: Putnam, 1991, 1996.

Folger, Liz. *The Stay-at-Home Mom's Guide to Making Money from Home.* Rev. 2nd ed. Roseville, CA: Prima Publishing, 2001.

Gault, Teri, with Sheryl Berk. *Shop Smart, Save More.* New York: HarperCollins, 2009.

Hamm, Trent. *365 Ways to Live Cheap! Your Everyday Guide to Saving Money.* Avon, MA: Adams Media, 2009.

Johnson, Tory, and Robyn Freedman Spizman. *Will Work From Home: Earn the Cash—Without the Commute.* New York: Penguin, 2008.

Karp, Gregory. *The 1-2-3 Money Plan.* Upper Saddle River, NJ: FT Press, 2009.

Karp, Gregory. *Living Rich by Spending Smart.* Upper Saddle River, NJ: Pearson Education, 2008.

Kay, Ellie. *1/2 Price Living: Secrets to Living Well on One Income.* Chicago: Moody, 2007.

Kay, Ellie. *The Little Book of Big Savings.* Colorado Springs, CO: Waterbrook Press, 2009.

McCoy, Jonni. *Miserly Moms: Living Well on Less in a Tough Economy.* 4th ed. Minneapolis, MN: Bethany, 2009.

Nelson, Stephanie. *The Coupon Mom's Guide to Cutting Your Grocery Bills in Half: The Strategic Shopping Method Proven to Slash Food and Drugstore Costs.* New York: Penguin, 2009.

Nelson, Stephanie. *Greatest Secrets of the Coupon Mom.* Los Angeles: DPL Press, 2005.

Ramsey, Dave. *The Total Money Makeover: A Proven Plan for Financial Fitness.* 2nd ed. Nashville, TN: Thomas Nelson, 2007.

Reader's Digest. *Free Money Free Stuff.* Pleasantville, NY: The Reader's Digest Association, Inc., 2007.

Rosenberg, Sharon Harvey. *The Frugal Duchess: How to Live Well and Save Money.* Los Angeles: DPL Press, 2008.

Sander, Peter, and Jennifer Sander. *573 Ways to Save Money*. Guilford, CT: The Lyons Press, 2009.

Sher, Barbara. *Refuse to Choose! Use All of Your Interests, Passions, and Hobbies to Create the Life and Career of Your Dreams*. Emmaus, PA: Rodale, 2007.

Winter, Barbara J. *Making a Living Without a Job: Winning Ways for Creating Work that You Love*. Rev ed. New York: Bantam, 2009.

Yeager, Jeff. *The Ultimate Cheapskate's Road Map to True Riches*. New York: Broadway Books, 2008.

Terms and Abbreviations to Know

When you first start looking for deals and communities online, you'll run across a lot of "insider" jargon, acronyms, and abbreviations. Use this handy guide to help you decipher the code.

AY. *All You* magazine. Sold at Walmart or by subscription and generally contains quite a few coupons.

blinkies. Manufacturer coupons dispensed by machines placed on a shelf in the store. Named for the little attention-getting blinking light on the machines.

blogroll. A list of a blogger's own favorite blogs, usually found in the sidebar of his or her blog.

BM (or B&M). *brick and mortar.* Physical (as opposed to online) stores.

BOGO. *buy one, get one free.* Sometimes written "B1G1." If you see B2G2, that means "buy two, get two free," and so on.

Catalina. A coupon printed by a separate machine at the register after you purchase particular items that trigger a particular coupon. Named after the company that makes and maintains the machines, the Catalina Corporation.

cherry-picking. Purchasing only the best deals at a given store or going from store to store to buy only the best deals at each.

couponer. Someone who uses coupons.

CRT. *cash register tape*. Often used as shorthand for coupons that print out right on a receipt.

dh. *dear husband*. Mommy blogger and forum shorthand. Also: dd (dear daughter), ds (dear son), ds6 (dear son 6 years old), and so on.

ECB. *Extra (Care) Bucks*. The coupons that print out at CVS and can be used like cash on your next purchase.

envie. *envelope*. Usually used in terms such as "I'll mail you an envie of coupons."

GM. *General Mills*. Used in reference to an occasional special coupon insert for GM products.

hangtags. Coupons that hang from the necks of products in the store.

IP. *internet printable*. Coupons you can print from the internet and use in a physical store.

K. *Kellogg's*. Used in reference to the back-to-school coupon insert at the end of the summer for Kellogg's products.

lurk. To join an online community but not actively participate; to watch without commenting.

mfr. *manufacturer* (as in *mfr. coupon*).

MIR. *mail-in rebate*.

newbie. Someone who is new to a given online community.

OOP. *out of pocket*. The amount of actual cash you spend on a given transaction at the store.

overage. The happy situation that occurs when you are able to use a coupon worth more than the price of the product, giving you "extra" toward the rest of the items in your order. (For example, if an item is on sale for 70 cents, and you have a $1-off coupon, you'll get 30 cents in *overage*.) Remember that overage is a privilege; many stores have a policy of adjusting coupon amounts down to the actual item price, and they are within their rights to do so.

OYNO. *on your next order.* Refers to a coupon you can use as cash on your next shopping trip.

OYNSO. *on your next shopping order.* See **OYNO.**

peelies. Coupons that are stuck onto a product; you "peel" these off in order to use them.

PG. *Procter & Gamble.* Used in reference to the P&G coupon insert, generally found in Sunday newspapers on a monthly basis.

PP. *participating products.*

Q. *coupon.*

roll. To use a Catalina (or Extra Bucks or Register Rewards) to purchase more Catalina-producing items.

RP. *RedPlum.* Coupon insert found in many Sunday newspapers.

RR. *Register Rewards.* Coupons that print out at Walgreens and can be used almost like cash to pay for your next order.

SAHM. *stay-at-home mom.*

SS. *SmartSource.* Coupon insert found in many Sunday newspapers.

stack. To layer your savings. In terms of coupons, it stands for layering more than one kind of savings on a single product, for instance, a manufacturer coupon plus a store coupon. In Catalina terms, it means that you can do a deal more than once in a single transaction. If you see an announcement of a "buy $30 of participating products, get $15" Catalina deal, and you can buy $60 of participating products at one time and get $30 back, the deal *stacks.*

tearpads. Coupons that you tear off of a pad, usually found by displays in-store.

V. *Valassis.* Sunday coupon insert. In most places, Valassis is the same as RedPlum (*see* **RP**).

WAHM. *work-at-home mom.*

WYB. *when you buy.*

YMMV. *your mileage may vary.* Means that a deal depends on certain factors that need to be in place for it to work.

About the Author

Rachel Singer Gordon, also known as Mashup Mom, is a former librarian who is now mashing up a new career as a freelance writer, editor, blogger, and workshop leader. She has written several books for librarians, but her most recent, *What's the Alternative? Career Options for Librarians and Info Pros* (2008, Information Today, Inc.), really made her think about how we can succeed with at-home work when we mash in those savings strategies. She frequently presents at conferences for info pros on topics such as generational issues and alternative careers, teaches coupon classes in the Chicagoland area, and has written for *The Dollar Stretcher*, a popular publication on saving money.

Rachel blogs on money-saving and money-making strategies at her popular deal blog, MashupMom.com (www.mashupmom.com). Email her at rachel@mashupmom.com.

Index